Grappa – Italy bottled

By Ove Boudin

ORIGINAL TITLE:
Grappa – Italien på flaska

PHOTOGRAPHY:
All pictures by Ove Boudin*

ENGLISH TRANSLATION:
Megan Lynch, and the author

GRAPHIC DESIGN AND LAYOUT:
Anders Wallin

ILLUSTRATIONS:
Eva Lilja

ISBN-13
978-91-633-1351-6

All rights reserved. No part of the content of this book may be reproduced without the written permission of the author or the publisher.

Copyright © 2007 PianoForte Publishing, Partille, Sweden.

www.lagrappa.eu

Printed in 2007 by Billes Tryckeri AB, Box 304, 431 24 Mölndal, Sweden.

* except for pictures on p. 104 supplied by Dist. Nardini and p. 147 by Maurizio Fava.

GRAPPA
Italy bottled

by

OVE BOUDIN

PianoForte Publishing

CONTENT
Grappa – Italy bottled

L'autunno
The autumn – Introduction   7

La Scuola – The school
1. A short lesson in wine and grapes   18
2. Vinaccia – a delicate matter   30
3. Distillation   36
4. Dilution and ageing   46
5. Grappa by definition   48
6. What is in a grappa   50
7. Classification and grappa varieties   52
8. Wine tasting   54
9. Grappa tasting   56
10. A splash of distillation history   66

Il Viaggio – The journey   75
Trentino –Alto Adige   79
Veneto/Friuli –Venezia Giulia   94
Tuscany   126
Liguria   135
Piemonte   143

References, sources and acknowledgements   164

List of grappa distilleries   166

DURING MY GRAPPA JOURNEY I actually visited twentyfour distilleries and had contact with about half a dozen more. They make up about a fourth of all Italy's grappa distilleries in the full sense of the word. Why I happened to visit exactly these was to a large extent a matter of chance, or fate if you wish. Perhaps it could have been possible to visit *all* distilleries, but such an enterprise is not necessary in order to communicate what distinguishes all who work for the good grappa – namely the passion and the respect for the tradition, the craftsmanship and the raw material. And that is what this book is mainly about and it is to these men and women I dedicate it – although only a few of them happen to be in my story. However, in the end of the book you will find a comprehensive list with the names, addresses and contact information of nearly all the distilleries in the grappa regions of Italy.

The grappa regions of Italy
Trentino-Alto Adige, Veneto, Friuli-Venezia Giulia, Lombardy, Piemonte

"Follow through your dream to the end
dig the seagull fly across the sky
to build its nest in the ferris wheel"
Donovan Leitch

L'autunno

THE AUTUMN

The best grappa is made in the autumn.

When the grapes are ripe and plump.

When the vines have soaked up the elements and minerals that are unique to the location and let them emerge in the grape skins.

When wine growers harvest the grapes, crush them and set the must for fermentation.

When the pressed grape skins are at their freshest.

When the steam rises white from the distillerys' chimneys and the master distillers contemplate and tinker to unlock the finest grappa. And practicing a tradition with roots in the ancient arts, medieval alchemy and natural science.

Still there are people that do not like grappa at all.

A small distillate with a big flavour
It is often said that grappa is just made from old leftovers – stalks and all. This boldly spoken *just* is often used to demonstrate knowledge but actually shows prejudice. Grappa is made from grape skins and seeds, not waste. It is about using the same grapes that the wine maker has just used.

There are three typically expressed reasons why people who otherwise enjoy wine and alcoholic liquors purport to dislike grappa:
- They have heard that grappa does not have a pleasant taste.
- They have tasted grappa they did not like and then as a result decided that all grappa must taste bad.
- They have never tasted a good grappa.

The last point is the most poignant. Grappa is an exclusive drink. Of every thousand bottles of spirituous liquors produced around the world, only one is a grappa.

Outside of Italy's borders, the selection is limited. This makes it difficult to have a true and accurate picture of grappa.

And grappa does not have just *one* flavour. In fact, no other distilled drink offers such a diverse and varied palate as grappa.

There is nothing like grappa
Grappa is a unique drink. The term "grappa" is protected by both EU and Italian law. No distillate outside of Italy's border may use the term grappa.

Grappa has its own world of aromas and flavours. When you drink grappa you should not expect a liqueur, whiskey or Cognac experience. You must free yourself from these patterns; have no expectations, just open your mind.

White grappa is the only distillate that gets its aroma and flavour from grapes only. Other distillates get their flavour, and colour, to a great extent from ageing in wooden barrels, post distillation. An aged grappa also gets its colour and some of its flavours in this way.

Grappa is made from a solid – pressed grape skins. All other alcoholic products of importance are distilled from a liquid raw material.

The raw material is a repeatedly recycled resource. After distilling, it becomes either fuel or is refined to make cooking oil and other useful products.

A cultural beverage
Grappa is Italian culture and history in liquid form. Unlike its many fine cousins around Europe – especially France – grappa was not born from a castle or named after a noble domain. Grappa has taken the long road. From the beginning it was more a kind of food than a beverage; something that could provide body heat, and also some relief in the misery.

Grappa's high status today is a result of better distilling methods, but mostly because of the industry's conscious marketing and product development since the 70's and 80's.

However, grappa is still a cultural drink. Grappa has a soul that has carried it through the ages; its quintessence or its core that makes grappa, grappa. It is essential that this is preserved.

A national asset
Grappa is a cultural beverage; and to sell grappa is to give the market the promise of inclusion in this culture. Everyone that produces and markets grappa therefore shares a responsibility to offer a grappa that upholds this promise. Even the Italian Government has a responsibility, as grappa is a national asset and brand that otherwise could get washed-out and loose its value. Today, there are about 135 grappa distilleries. In 1900, there were 100,000.

What is a distillery?
The reality is that most distilleries do not distil. Apart from the real distilleries there are around 500 so-called bottlers who acquire the raw material and then let a real distillery distil, age and bottle the grappa according to their instructions. Other bottlers buy finished grappa and then blend, bottle and market the grappa themselves under their own label. Then there are a large number of distributors, farms, restaurants and other companies that put their own labels on finished grappa. Many of these companies call themselves distilleries.

Real distilleries have chimneys with white smoke coming out, preferably in the autumn.

The two schools of distilling
Grappa is either produced in industrial distilleries or in boutique distilleries. The industrial-scale distilleries represent only one fifth of all distilleries but are responsible for four fifths of the total output. Just one company, Distillerie Bonollo (Italy's largest producer of all categories of industrial spirits) produces almost half of all the industrially distilled grappa, i.e. about 40 percent of Italy's total grappa production.

Of course, boutique distilleries have greater possibilities to create more traditional and diverse grappa than industrial distillers. Some aficionados and purists (who only accept boutique grappa) are of the opinion that industrial distillers are a threat to the future of true grappa. However, both distillery schools have their different roles that in the big-picture presuppose each other's existence.

Industrial grappa

The role of the industrial distilleries is to provide the world with grappa. Volume production and efficiency are key words here. Industrial-scale grappa is made from not only fresh grape skins, but also grape skins that have been stored for a period of time. Due to the production techniques, industrial grappa has a more neutral flavour. But industrial distilleries can still deliver a good, consistent-quality grappa.

However the attitude towards the distilling methods differ. Some producers speak openly about their industrial process *(a continuo)*, while others emphasize tradition, heritage and even artisan technique *(a discontinuo)*, although their grappa is mass produced. And it is not unusual for distilleries to top up their own production with grappa from other industrial producers. Some big distilleries though actually have smaller stills to create boutique grappa in limited editions. Some use them anyhow merely as captivating viewing models for visitors.

Boutique grappa
The artisan distiller's role is more about bringing a tradition to life and illustrate how grappa "should really" taste. The activity revolves around the master distiller's passion and the art of creating grappa.

The best boutique distilleries always use fresh grape skins and are able to adjust the output to the supply of grapes. The result is an authentic grappa with characteristics unique to the distiller. This grappa can be very rough and rustic – more difficult to approach in other words, but of an excellent quality.

The customer has a right to know
What makes a great grappa is ultimately determined by the customers. Selling grappa also implies a duty to "educate" and develop the awareness of

consumers. This presupposes transparency and openness from producers. Customers have the right to kwow what they are buying. When, where, of what, by whom and by which method is the grappa made? Today, there are not enough labelling requirements to ensure that detailed information is consistently provided. The manufacturers themselves determine to a large extent what should appear on the bottle.

A declaration of goods of this kind would be beneficial for the smaller artisan distillers as they could lay claim to certain quality concepts as *discontinuo* (batchwise production). The industrial distilleries could offer this as they have the resources, the advantage and a global market. And a stronger focus on the quality of grappa would increases the interest in grappa and consequently the market.

This scenario would benefit all grappa producers.

Now, how should grappa taste?
There was a time when grappa was a challenge that made me hesitate. Then the challenge aroused my curiosity. Here was a drink that did not egg me on, saying *drink me* but was more contrary and unfavourably disposed towards me. This attitude felt liberating and I decided to like grappa. I realised pretty quickly that this cool attitude was only a way to hide a secret – like an entry test before getting into the club.

But I still could not make head or tail of grappa. No matter how many varieties of grappa I tried, the grappa continued to baffle me. One day I asked my youngest daughter, when she visited Turin, to go in search of a specialist grappa seller and see what they recommended. When even *that grappa* confused my senses, I realised that the fault was hardly with the grappa.

I decided to go in search of the soul of grappa. In October 2005 I travelled to Italy and during two months I visited 24 distilleries in the regions of Trentino-Alto Adige, Veneto, Friuli-Venezia Giulia, Tuscany, Liguria and Piemonte.

Now, how should grappa taste?

It should taste of where it was made.

An experience hidden in an aroma
When the grapes grow, the flavour of earth is transferred to the grape skins and finally to the wine and grappa. That is why different locations have their own flavours and scents that may be identified in a wine or a grappa, in fruit and vegetables, maybe even in some food. This local flavour, together with the distiller's talents and preferences, affect the finished grappa.

When travelling we are somehow more open to new taste sensations that can have deep and lasting effects – so deep that a similar experience many years later can momentarily pull you back to that time and place. Memories can be bottled in an aroma.

Similarly, other sensory impressions can enrich a grappa and come to life much later. My scent-memories from some distilleries are especially strong – something similar to boiling jam from berries. However, even the mountain slopes, hills and fields affect the experience of a grappa. As do the quiet changing autumn colours, the landscape's mood and the wonderful people you meet.

But I understood none of this until I had arrived at home again.

The perfect ending
Grappa – Italy bottled is really two books in one. The first contains everything you need to know about grappa. The second is the story of my journey. Hopefully my book will have you yearning for Italy and start planning your own trip. But take your own route. It may seem like my journey was planned, but it

was more of an improvisation with a little help from above. Fortunately you do not have to repeat this feat. *Grappa – Italy bottled* also contains a comprehensive list of real distilleries in the grappa regions of Italy. However, the mere fact that you will be travelling in Italy is no guarantee that you will be served or find good grappa everywhere, especially of course in non-grappa regions.

Grappa is never obvious, not even in Italy.

One piece of advice – try to learn some Italian before you go. It sounds pretentious but through the language you get closer to the locals and the grappa. For me the language has become an ingredient in grappa as much as the aromas of the grapes and my own experiences.

And grappa tastes better if your order it in the language of grappa. *Cameriere! Voremmo due caffè e due grappe, per favore. Grappe nostrane naturalmente!*

Grappa is the perfect way to finish off dinner – which for too long and for too many has been the forgotten star in *la cucina italiana*.

La scuola

THE SCHOOL

A short lesson in wine and grapes

Wine and grappa share a common origin – grapes. Both the quality of wine and grappa therefore depends heavily on the variety or blend of varieties, where they are grown and the treatment during production. Careful and thoughtful handling is the underpinning of any quality wine, which also carries over into grappa's raw material.

A single grape variety can have different characteristics depending on where the grape stock is grown. Wine aficionados call this the *terroir effect*. *Terroir* comprises climate, location and soil, and is used when explaining a special character of a wine from a specific region or area.

Climate and Location
The best wine growing regions are found in between the latitudes of 30 to 50 degrees from the equator in both the northern and southern hemispheres. The further away from the equator the wine is grown the more concentrated the aromas and flavour. The grapes have to fight harder to survive. Hard winters also give the vines an opportunity to rest and gather strength. Conversely, the warmer the climate, the harder it is to create a truly good wine. The vines produce fruit year round and never have an opportunity to rest. The risks of tropical rain and fungal infections are also more prevalent.

Grapes require lots of sun, as it is the heat of the sun that builds up the sugar content of the grape. In the northern hemisphere, the best growing aspect is a southern facing slope. Naturally, the difficulty for wine growers in colder regions is a lack of sun and the risk of frost and hail damage to the harvest.

Cembra valley, Trentino.

Soil Quality

Soil and drainage affect a grape's flavour and characteristics. The soil temperature, more than the air temperature, affects the growth of the vine. Well-drained soil is warmer than soil with a higher moisture content. The ideal location for grape vines is half-way up a slope where there is good drainage and the vines can take best advantage of the sun's rays.

Gravel soil is the driest and warmest soil and can be found most often on the slopes of river valleys. For example, Cabernet Sauvignon grows best in Médoc's dry hills in Bordeaux.

Chalky earth high in lime provides good drainage that forces the vine's roots deep into the soil to tap into a stable water supply. Grapevines are one of the few plants that absorb minerals from the soil. Chardonnay for example prefers an alkyline soil which results in fresh, mineral-rich wines, such as those in the Chablis and Champagne regions.

Granite in the soil, commonly found in regions such as the Rhône Valley and Beaujolais, both reflects and absorbs the sun's rays and is an important component of some of the great red wines. Rocky soil makes life difficult for the grapevines contributing to a more concentrated grape flavour.

Soils high in shale are rich in minerals with the dark shale stones absorbing the sun's energy and giving the soil the warmth the grapevine requires. This kind of soil can be found in the Mosel-Saar-Ruwer-region.

It is important that micro-organisms such as fungi, algae and bacteria are present in the soil as it encourages the absorption of minerals from the earth through the roots of the grapevines. Even worms, snails and insects are important as they help aerate and break up the soil.

Harvest time

The spring blossoms first appear approximately twelve weeks after the first buds and blossom for about two weeks. Then come the important "one hundred days", when all the crucial elements combine – rain, but not too much and birds must be kept at bay so that the sun's warmth can transform the hard fruit into juicy grapes. As the grapes ripen, the acidity of the grapes falls while the sweetness increases. The autumn approaches and the harvest season nears. The percentage of grape must (juice) is measured. And the eternal question for the wine growers occurs – do we dare to wait an extra day to harvest or will rain, storms or frost get there before? When the optimal balance between sweetness and acidity is reached, the grapes are harvested in the shortest time frame possible.

In colder wine growing regions like Canada, Germany and Austria, the grapes are sometimes not harvested until the first frost. This process increases the sugar content of the grapes and produces sweeter wines such as *Eiswein* (literally translated means ice wine).

Fine wine-quality grapes are harvested by hand, so that only the best and unbroken grapes are collected. This is important, as grapes that are over-ripe or damaged begin to ferment and oxidise from contact with the air. For this reason it is vital that the grapes are harvested quickly and the vinification process is started as soon as possible. The freshness of the grapes is the be all and end all of a good wine.

Wine growers talk about the three different climates of vineyards: macro, meso and microclimates. Macroclimate includes factors such as the vineyard's gradient of slope and proximity to the ocean. Mesoclimate encompasses factors which are more particular to the vineyard such as its position in relation to lakes, rivers etc. Microclimate includes those aspects which affect the foliage. The microclimate can be affected by trellising the vines. Binding and supporting the vines with trellising encourages air circulation, reduces the spread of plant diseases and help position the grapes for maximum sun exposure. The pictures show typical "trellisings" at vineyards in Mezzocorona and Cembra valley in Trentino.

WINE MAKING

The quality of the wine is a reflection of the wine maker's skill. This includes skills such as the choice of grape and treatment, production equipment, the choice of fermentation temperature and fermentation timing, filtration and storage methods as well as many other talents. The vinification – the process of making wine – is carried out in four steps: the crush, the fermenting of the must, the bottling and the storage.

Alcohol fermentation

Yeast exists naturally on the skin of grapes. When fissures or cracks occur on grape skins the yeast comes in contact with the sweet grape juice and an uncontrolled process begins. These so-called "wild" yeast cultures are not usually enough for a complete fermentation process of wine and therefore yeasts with known properties are added. Controlled fermentation of the grapes and skins is a time-honoured concept in all wine and grappa making processes.

Through the fermentation process the yeast transforms the fructose (fruit sugars) into alcohol, carbon dioxide and heat. The more fructose that is fermented, the drier and less sweet the wine becomes and vice versa.

Producing white wine

The newly harvested grapes are gently crushed in a wine press. The resulting must is separated from the skins and stalks which are removed from the process and the pure must is pumped into a stainless steel tank. As the stalks and skins are not present, a cultured yeast is added to the must to begin the fermentation process – which can take anywhere from a few days to a couple of weeks depending on the type of wine.

To reduce oxidisation and unwanted fermentation, sulphur dioxide is added. You might notice a slight hint of sulphur that quickly dissipates from a newly opened bottle of wine.

When the yeast has done its work and transformed the fructose into alcohol it dies, building up sediment in the wine. Most wines go through a filtration process to remove the sediment.

A side-effect of this process is that some aroma-giving substances in the wine are also filtered away. As a consequence some wine makers skip this process.

If the fructose content is too low, sugar can be added to increase the alcohol content (chaptalising). On the other hand if the acidity is too low, tartaric acid can be added (acidifying).

To conclude the process the wine is stored and subsequently bottled.

Method Champagnois

Champagne is created when the wine is allowed an additional fermentation process in the bottle by adding extra yeast and must. During fermentation, carbon dioxide builds up and as it cannot escape anywhere, the wine becomes carbonated or "bubbly"! The bottles are tilted slightly forward so that the neck of the bottle points down slightly. This is to catch any sediment that forms during the second fermentation. Then the neck of the bottle is frozen to allow the cork and the frozen sediment plug to be removed. The bottle is filled up with a little wine and finally sealed with a new cork and wire fastenings. *Voila!*

The cellar of the wine maker Azienda Agricola Accornero, also including an agriturismo, in Vignale Monferrato, Piemonte.

Producing red wine

The red grapes are gently crushed in a wine press in much the same way as the green grapes and everything: the must, the grape skins – and sometimes even the stalks depending on the sort of wine – are pumped into a fermentation tank.

As a rule, red wine has two fermentations. During the first fermentation – alcohol fermentation – the important *maceration* takes place: colour pigment and tannin from the grape skins permeate the grape must. This is how red wine gets its red-colour. Grape juice is naturally colourless. Alcohol fermentation occurs in both the must and the grape skins, and eventually even in the other more solid substances.

Tannins are an acidic substance found in grape's skins and stalks. Tannic acid gives the wine its strength and power and is a prerequisite for the long-term storage of a wine.

Next, the fermented mixture is gently filtered: the skins and solids are removed and the pinkish purple wine is pumped into a vat for the second fermentation. During this second fermentation, called the *malolatic* fermentation or MLF, the malic acid in the wine is transformed into lactic acid with the assistance of bacteria. This metamorphosis reduces the acidity and enhances the body of the wine and improves its ageing properties.

Afterwards the wine is allowed to rest in barrels before eventual bottling.

However, if the skins had been removed after the first crush to let the must alone ferment, the result would have been a white wine – even if the grapes were red. In fact, Champagne is made from a two-thirds blend of red grapes.

In contrast to the majority of white wines, most red wines are a blend of various grapes.

Ageing – storage and cellaring

All the top-class wines are stored in oak barrels. This contributes to the colour of the wine and adds both noble taste like vanilla but also tannic acid. Even some white wines are stored in oak barrels. However the majority of wines are stored in stainless steel tanks.

A vat – also known as *barrique*, is a barrel that

most commonly holds 225 litres. Previously, many different sorts of wood including chestnut, cherry and acacia trees were used in the construction of a barrel; however, today almost all barrels for quality wines are made from oak. Oak is very strong as well as water-tight and complements the wine in an almost magical way. The newer the vat, the more flavour it will give to the wine. Roasting the barrel also affects the oak flavour and tannins in the wine. After using an oak vat three times, the oak flavour is almost completely exhausted.

White wine is stored in oak vats for approximately 6-8 months. Red wine is stored longer and can remain in the barrel for anywhere between 9 to 18 months depending on the wine maker's specifications.

Rosé wine

Rosé is distilled in much the same way as white wine, however a rosé must briefly be in contact with the red grape skins before fermentation. The longer the contact, the stronger the colour of the wine. One way to create rosé wine is to simply add red wine that has not finished fermenting into the white must.

Sweet wines

To produce a fine sweet wine, e.g. *Sauternes* from Bordeaux, only the grapes that have been allowed to shrivel on the vine in a controlled manner are used. Given the right weather conditions, the sugar, acid and aroma of the grapes will increase as the size of the grape decreases.

Eiswein is produced from frozen grapes that during the crush exude a sweet syrup-like juice and leave behind the frozen crystallised water molecules.

It is also possible to increase the sweetness by sun-drying the grapes. *Amarone* wine from Italy is created through this method.

Fortified wines

If alcohol is added to the vinification or wine making process, the yeast is killed and fermentation ceases. The alcohol transforms the wine into fortified wine. If the alcohol is added before the fermentation is complete, there will still be sugar remaining – hence it becomes a sweet fortified wine. Naturally, if the alcohol is added after the fermentation is finished the result is a dry fortified wine.

Something wrong with the wine?

If the wine:

- Tastes mouldy like an old cellar – there is a problem with the cork. Cork is a natural material that contains micro-organisms and is therefore sterilised with chlorine. Sometimes traces of the chlorine remain and can spoil a wine. Box wine and synthetic corks do not affect the wine.
- Tastes like "burnt matchstick" – a smell of sulphur dioxide. The sensation dissipates as the wine is allowed to breathe for a while. Extreme doses can destroy the wine.
- Smells like rotten egg – the sulphuric smell reveals that the wine is defective or produced in a faulty manner.
- Is brown or very yellow – the wine has oxidised, in other words, air has managed to get through the cork and has reacted with the tartaric acid and created vinegar. For this reason, wine should be cellared lying flat so that the cork does not dry out such that fissures form in the cork.
- Contains small white crystals – tartaric acid crystals form naturally and is a completely harmless sediment.

An apple with a bite taken out of it soon becomes unappetisingly brown. The oxygen in the air reacts with the apple in a process called oxidisation. In much the same way, grapes and the grape juice are prone to oxidisation – from harvesting and long into the wine process. Wine growers stave off oxidisation in various ways: they do not harvest during the hottest hours of the day; they pick and transport them carefully; and even add sulphur dioxide as an antioxidant in the wine.

THE VINE AND GRAPES

Good grapes are a requirement of a good wine. Creating a great wine begins at the growing stages.

A grape consists of skin, juice, seeds and stalk. The skin is most important, as it holds a wine's aroma, colour and tannins. Even the stalks contain tannins, but the stalks nowadays commonly are separated out prior to fermentation. Seeds also contain tannins but also bitter tasting oils. The flesh of the grape is mostly water.

A living grapevine produces fruit from the same location for approximately thirty years. There are thousands of varieties of grapevines with their own individual characteristics. Only a few will ever be involved in the wine making process. The majority of those grapes used belong to the species *Vitis vinifera*.

Common Green Grapes

CHARDONNAY
One of the world's most popular and most commonly grown grapes. At its best this grape has hints of nuts, butter, mushrooms and fruits like peaches and melon. Chardonnay is the only grape allowed in Chablis wines and is one of the three grapes in Champagne.

SAUVIGNON BLANC
Probably the most cultivated white wine grape after Chardonnay. This grape produces a light but full bodied wine with an aroma that is reminiscent of herbs and grapefruit.

RIESLING
An aromatic grape, Riesling is most commonly associated with the Mosel and Alsace regions. These wines have a characteristic perfume of honey, mineral and even petrol!

GEWÜRTZTRAMINER
A strongly aromatic grape, Gerwürtzraminer evokes a sensation of roses, ginger and cinnamon (*gewürtz* means spice in German). It is commonly blended with other grapes in regions such as Alsace, Germany, Switzerland, Austria and northern Italy

In late autumn to early winter, Luciano Agostinetto in Valdobbiadene fine-cuts his Prosecco grapevines and fertilises and aerates the soil for the next season. Single bunches of grapes hide here and there. Prosecco is nowadays trademarked and may only be stated on wines from Veneto, more specifically the region Conegliano/Valdobbiadene.

The grapevine's enemy number one is Grape Phylloxera (Phylloxera vastatrix) – a louse that attacks the root system of the grapevine and restrict its ability to absorb nutrients from the soil. There is no known cure, however the effects can be slowed or retarded by grafting. Originally, Phylloxera came from North America and devastated European viniculture from the end of the 1800's and long into the 1900's. Root systems from the Vitis Labrusca (an American grape vine which is immune to the effects of Phylloxera) were successfully grafted with the European Vitis Vinifera grape vines.

where it is called *Traminer Aromatico*. The grape is considered to have its origins in the north Italian village of Traminer.

MÜLLER-THURGAU
This grape has a smooth rounded flavour and a hint of acidity. Müller-Thurgau is commonly used in German wine blends. It is also commonly grown in Austria, Hungary, Czech Republic and Croatia.

MUSCAT
Muscat is one of the oldest and most aromatic grape varieties. Grown all over the world, this grape is most often used to create sweet dessert wines but can be found in various wines from rose scented wines of Alsace to sparkling *spumante* wine from Asti in Piemonte.

PINOT BLANC
Pinot Blanc creates a full-bodied but less aromatic wine. It is grown in north-eastern Italy, Austria, Croatia, Slovenia, Hungary and Romania.

PINOT GRIS
Often grown in Alsace, Germany and Austria, this grape produces fine wines with spicy tones and a slight acidity. In Italy this grape is known as Pinot Grigio and is most commonly found in the north-eastern regions of the country.

Common Red Grapes

BARBERA
This is one of Italy's most commonly grown grapes. Particularly popular in Piemonte, it gives that characteristic fullness and fruitiness to the wines of the region.

CABERNET SAUVIGNON
Probably the world's most well known and most cultivated grape. Cabernet Sauvignon is a tannin-rich grape that delivers a powerful aroma of black-currant as well as a capacity for long cellaring. It is grown all over Italy and is a component of some of Tuscany's most famous wines.

DOLCETTO
Another tannin-rich wine, this grape is ruby red and grown almost exclusively in Piemonte, where only Barbera and Nebbiolo are more common. The aroma from Dolcetto is reminiscent of sweet berries or plums.

MERLOT
A classic grape, Merlot is often blended with Cabernet Sauvignon. The characteristic aromas of a Merlot wine are dark berries, vanilla, caramel and spices. It is also common in the classified wines of Tuscany.

NEBBIOLO
One of Italy's most distinguished grapes; it is the base for wines such as Barbaresco and Barolo from Piemonte. Nebbiolo has a bouquet of roses, tea leaves, spices and tar. Thanks to the full tannins of the grape, the wine can be cellared for long periods. The name comes from the word *nebbia* – the legendary winter mists of northern Italy.

PINOT NOIR
The most important grape for red Bourgogne wines, it is also called *Pinot Nero*, *Pignola*, or pale-red Burgundy (Spät- or Blauburgunder). It is difficult to grow and gives wines an aroma of roses, raspberries and cherries.

SANGIOVESE
The most cultivated red grape in Italy, Sangiovese is the base of many famous Tuscan wines such as Brunello di Montalcino and Chianti. The late-maturing grapes produce elegant wine of lighter fullness and an aroma of red berries.

SYRAH
A tannin-rich grape, Syrah is a full-bodied wine with an aroma of blackberries, black currants and raisins. It is also known as *Shiraz* in Australia.

A HISTORY OF WINE THROUGH ITALIAN EYES

The art of wine making is ancient. Actually, it is not an art, as wine is created when the grape juice comes in contact with the outer skin of the grape. The earliest reference to wine making comes from the Caucasus, in modern-day Iran, somewhere between 6,000 to 7,000 years ago. In the ancient Egypt of the Pharaohs, the methods used to ferment wine were refined and the art of wine making spread to Greece. From around 1,000 BC until 500 BC, the Greeks colonised large parts of the Mediterranean and with them came viniculture. Southern Italy became the Greeks' vineyard and over time Pompeii became the ancient world's wine centre.

The eruption of Vesuvius in 79 AD buried Pompeii but also contributed to the diversification of wine commerce and by 200 AD wine was grown throughout the Roman Empire. The Romans established vineyards in many European regions including Rioja, Garonne, Champagne and Bourgogne, as well as in the Mosel and Danube Valleys, to provide supplies for their legions.

The fall and resurrection

The fall of the Roman Empire was catastrophic for the European wine industry. This was especially the case for Italy, where viniculture lost its status and was almost forgotten. It wasn't until the 13th and 14th centuries that wine trade became successful once again for the larger trading cities of Genoa, Venice and Florence. In Bordeaux, Bourgogne, Rhine and Danube exports were booming. It was however France, Germany, Spain and Portugal that were at the forefront of the resurrection of wine and its popularity, whereas Italy would lag behind for some time still.

Pitigliano, the old Tuscan city that seem to emerge from the limestone rock.

The golden age

During the 18th and 19th centuries there was great progress in the wine regions, most of all for France where classifications of wine from Médoc and Sauternes in Bordeaux were introduced and are still in use to this day. However, it was not until the beginning of the 1800's that this progress reached Italy. It was Piemonte and Tuscany that first adopted the new ways and world renowned wines as Barolo, Brunello and Chianti were created. The wine houses like Gancia, Martini and Cinzano were born and the San Michele wine growers institute was established in Trentino.

Another collapse and boom

The phylloxera plague and two world wars hit the burgeoning trend in Italian wines and changed the direction of the industry. Difficult times sparked a move by many wine growers towards volume production and the focus moved to those grapes that returned the greatest possible yield. Wine was not viewed as a luxury item but instead as everyday common-fare, rich in calories. It was not until the 1960's that consumer attitudes changed, with the focus changing to quality rather than quantity. Consumption rates dropped and the demand for quality wine increased.

The boom began in Tuscany with the production of high-quality table wine from the French grape varieties such as Cabernet Sauvignon, Merlot, Chardonnay and Syrah, which were stored in oak barrels. Piemonte followed the Tuscan example and adapted their Barolo and Barbera wines to better suit the international markets.

Developments in viniculture had until this point in time focused on the production of wine, however by the 1990's more attention was focused on wine growing methods, which led to the establishment of a new wine category *Indicazione Geografica Tipica (IGT)* – officially approved wines that are representative of their geographic region. In later years, Italian wine growers have also begun to show interest in lesser-known and unexploited native grape varieties.

Classification and approved-regional wines of Italy

- VdT – *Vini da tavola* – table wines without a precise origin or vintage
- IGT – *Indicazione Geografica Tipica* – table wines from a specified region, grape variety, style and vintage
- DOC – *Denominazione di Origine Controllata* – quality controlled wines with a certification of origin, registered grape varieties and winemaking methods.
- DOCG – *Denominazione di Origine Controllata e Garantita* – quality assured and guaranteed wines with certifications such as *Riserva*, *Superiore* and *Classico*.

Examples of DOCG wines

DOCG-certified	Region	Primary grape variety
Asti	Piemonte	Muscat
Barbaresco	Piemonte	Nebbiolo
Barolo	Piemonte	Nebbiolo
Brunello di Montalcino	Toscana	Sangiovese
Chianti	Toscana	Sangiovese
Chianti Classico	Toscana	Sangiovese
Vino nobile di Montepulciano	Toscana	Sangiovese

500 kg (1100 lb) of fresh grapes produces 420 kg (920 lb) of wine must and 80 kg (175 lb) of vinaccia.

- 100 kg (220 lb) vinaccia contains:
  - 65-70 kg (150 lb) grape skins
  - 30-35 kg (75 lb) seeds

(Stalks, if any, are removed before distillation. Today most wineries separate the stalks prior to fermentation.)

- 100 kg (220 lb) *vinaccia* (5% alkohol) produces around 5 litres of grappa (100% alcohol).
- In other words: 1 bottle of grappa requires vinaccia from approximately 50 bottles of wine.
- Yearly production of wine grapes in Italy: 7,5 million tonnes.
- Total vinaccia: 1,2 million tonnes.
- Total vinaccia used to produce grappa: 0.3 million tonnes.
- Yearly production of grappa (40% vol.): circa 44 million bottles (700 ml).

Vinaccia – a delicate matter

Vinaccia is the grape solids from which grappa is derived. The suffix *accia* reveals that there is a negative undertone to this word. A linguist would say that the suffix *accia* has a pejorative (negative) meaning. *Il vino* is the useful and enjoyable wine, whereas *la vinaccia* is the waste bi-products of wine production – the grape skins, fruit fibre, seeds and stalks, if any. It is also known as pomace and sometimes marc.

However, for a grappa maker the vinaccia is far more than the poor, left-over solids. It is the beginning of everything. Vinaccia is the foundation of the unique sensory code behind grappa. It does not matter how accomplished, experienced or passionate a *maestro (master)* distiller is – or how refined the distillation equipment *il alambicco* is. It is impossible to get a good grappa out of bad vinaccia. A grappa's characteristic aroma and flavour has its origin in the grapes and cannot be added before, during or after the distillation process.

The vineyard – the origin of grappa
The quality of the vinaccia is dependent on many factors, such as the grape variety, where it is grown and how it is harvested, transported and handled during the wine-making process – but most importantly how the vinaccia is treated afterwards, up until the distillation.

As wine and grappa have a common raw material *materia prima*, good grapes for the wine maker are also good grapes for the grappa distiller. When wine growers take advantage of the geographic location and soil, they also contribute to the quality of the grappa.

However, the wine maker has an even greater influence on a grappa during the pressing of the grapes. The grapes must be crushed using balanced pressure, so that not all the sugar and alcohol-rich must is pressed out. The last drops are of little use to either wine or grappa. A top class vinaccia is a rich, aromatic and moist pulp. Grappa and its cousins in other countries, are the only alcoholic drinks of importance that are created from a solid, non-liquid raw material.

Grappa is the only distillate among the great alcoholic drinks in the world that is distilled directly from a solid raw material.

Specially constructed sacks for storage of vinaccia in a middle-size industry. The carbon dioxide that is released as the grape solids begin to ferment pushes out the oxygen and protects the raw material against oxidisation.

Cement silos for long-time storage of vinaccia.

A container with a batch of fresh vinaccia that is distilled almost instantly.

Oxygen is a bad partner

The most critical time for the vinaccia is the period between vinification and distillation. It should be as short as possible. Vinaccia is a fresh material that contains energy, nutrients and oxygen as well as a great deal of alcohol – an environment also loved by micro organisms like bacteria, yeast and fungi. After only a day, the raw vinaccia can be beset by these micro organisms and the sensory profile can be altered. If unchecked, this fermentation process can produce acetic acid and methyl-alcohol, which encourages mould, and the raw material will rot.

The preservation of the vinaccia is a crucial factor – especially for the big distilleries that cannot distil all the vinaccia promptly. The problem is that the solids come in contact with the air and begin to oxidise and break down.

The very big distilleries store the vinaccia for several months in enormous, open cement silos. The vinaccia is covered with plastic tarpaulins with sand spread over the top to push out any air pockets. Some distilleries have developed oxygen-free storage and fermentation processes by replacing oxygen with carbon dioxide.

Vinaccia is therefore a delicate matter. Craftsmen from boutique distilleries say the small distilleries can produce a high quality grappa because they can begin processing the raw material immediately and preserve its freshness. The larger industrial distilleries do not contradict this, but they contend that their preserving and distilling methods compensate for the longer storage times.

Boutique distillers buy their raw material from local growers – or use vinaccia from their own wine production – reducing transport time and maintaining the quality of the vinaccia. Larger distilleries cannot meet their demands from only local growers and therefore must source their vinaccia from all over Italy.

VARIETIES OF VINACCIA

Fermented vinaccia
To distil the grape solids they must contain a certain level of alcohol. When vinaccia leaves the winery the solids are at various stages of fermentation depending on the type of wine the estate is producing. As a rule of thumb, the difference between red and white vinaccia is that during red wine production the grape skins ferment with the wine must so that the wine can draw out the colour, flavour and tannins. As the skins are depleted of their structure for the benefit of the wine, the vinaccia from red wine has a more neutral sensory tone – less aroma to give to the grappa. The fructose is exhausted and transformed into alcohol. A completely fermented vinaccia of this type has an alcohol content of around 3-6 percent and is distilled as is.

Half-fermented vinaccia
Vinaccia from rosé and lighter red wines has only fermented for a short time together with the must to transfer some colour from the grape skins. Only a part of the aroma in the skin has been transferred to the wine must and there is still a sizeable quantity of sugar left that has not been fermented into alcohol. This half-fermented vinaccia – made of both red and green grapes – the grappa distillery has to ferment further until it has an alcohol content between 2-4 percent.

Unfermented vinaccia
Vinaccia from white wine is called *vergine* – unfermented. The solids are separated immediately after the first crush and have never been in contact with the wine must. A vinaccia *vergine* contains all the sugar and all the original aromas of the grape – for the skilled grappa maker this represents a potential that can be taken advantage of. As the solids are not fermented, they must be fermented until almost all of the sugar is exhausted before distilling. The alcohol content then rises to around 2-4 percent.

Before fermentation any stalks are removed. They contain woody fibres and oil, which can give the grappa a bitter taste. However only a small part of today's vinaccia contain stalks, since they are commonly removed by the wine producers. The seeds also contain bitter oils that can get into the grappa. To avoid any of these oils releasing, the grapes are firstly carefully pressed to avoid crushing any seeds and secondly are distilled at a relatively low pressure and temperature.

GRAPE VARIETIES

The variety of grape is important for grappa but not as crucial as for a wine. Vinaccia from a good wine is no guarantee that the solids are of the best quality. The best harvest time for wine is not always the best for grappa. Many believe that the best grappa comes from those grapes with an early harvest period, as the solids will have a higher acidity. And the warmer the climate the more quickly the acidity of a grape will sink. This could be one of the reasons for the good reputation of northern Italian grappa.

Grappa can be produced from all grape varieties, however, some grapes have naturally higher sensory characteristics. This particularly includes the aromatic grape varieties like Muscat, Gewürztraminer, Riesling and Müller-Thurgau. Their typically fruity aromas are enough to flavour even grappa. Therefore grappas with clear and easily identifiable aromas are often regarded as suitable for the "beginner".

With other grappa it is almost impossible to define the grape variety, however this does not mean that it is of lesser quality. Quite the opposite. Instead it has a perfume and taste sensation that can take your thoughts and feelings in unexpected directions.

A *grappa monovitigno* is a grappa distilled from vinaccia of a single grape variety. If a distillery can show that a grappa is made up of a grape variety such as Muscat or Merlot grapes, they can called it a *Grappa Moscato* or *Grappa Merlot*. The risk of course is that grappa from well-known grape varieties may not meet consumer expectations based on wine experiences.

Generally, industrial distilleries produce grappa made of vinaccia from many sources and grape varieties. The larger production and efficiency requirements mean that it is very difficult to produce more specialised, short series of grappa. Medium to smaller sized distilleries can adapt their production to the supply of vinaccia. It is these smaller grappa distilleries that produce *grappa monovitigno*

A scarce product in large quantities

According to the Italian law all vinaccia must be distilled to make either grappa or another kind of spirit. However only one quarter of all the vinaccia from Italian wine production will ever become grappa. The rest is used to create industrial spirit. This is due to the fact that most grappa distilleries are located in Northern Italy and they are unable to use the fresh vinaccia from the south due to storage and transport issues.

The hot climate in Southern Italy is also a problem. The strong sun increases the sugar content of the grapes and creates the strong, full-bodied wines but it also reduces the tannic acid which is a natural preservative. The heat similarly accelerates the fermentation process during storage. Industry and academic bodies are intensely researching better ways to improve the storage of vinaccia. One reason for this research is to increase grappa production but also to encourage more distilleries to establish themselves in the South.

RECYCLING THE VINACCIA

Grapes can be used many times over. Firstly as wine, then as grappa and after this it can be used as fuel or as a raw material for other food industry products, such as cooking oil.

The high temperatures of the *alambicco* demand high levels of energy, however most distilleries are self-sufficient when it comes to energy, thanks to the grapes. Vinaccia is used to not only for the grappa but also fuels the distilling process – and warms the building during the distilling season.

Vinaccia is recycled in various ways depending on the distillation method and conditions. After distillation, around 40 percent of the grape solids' water content remains and must be removed before the vinaccia can be used as a fuel. Distilleries that use water vapour in their processes (either continuous or batchwise methods with steam) have to dry out the used vinaccia in rotating cylinders before the grape seeds can be separated. The dry grape solids are then used as fuel for the still's fires and the seeds are sold on to companies to refine.

The seeds, which contain wood and oil, then become cooking oil – *olio di vinacciolo* or *olio di semi d'uva* is popular due to its zero cholesterol and a high boiling point which allows safer frying. The oil is also used in skin products, colorants, pig and bird food, compost and energy pellets.

Distilleries that do not dry their vinaccia sell it as it is to companies for further refinement or use it for themselves as fertiliser and compost.

Some distilleries also sell the unwanted parts of the distallation process (the *testa* and *coda*) to chemical companies, which eventually will become, amongst other products, formaldehyde.

Drying used vinaccia.

Seeds being separated.

Steaming vinaccia waiting to be refined or reused as fertiliser.

Distillation

The Latin word *destillare* is made up of two parts: *de* meaning something which runs downwards and *stillare* which means to drip. To distil a liquid it is boiled and the steam vapour is then pulled off to cool and condense to become a liquid again. This method separates the liquid from a raw material, leaving a concentrate of substances. Grappa is a liquid that is distilled from fermented vinaccia.

The raw material contains various components with different boiling and condensation points – this makes it possible to separate the substances from each other. The reference point for the distillation of alcohol is 78.4°C or 172°F. This is the boiling point for *ethanol* (ethyl alcohol) – the most important alcohol in the distillate.

Head, heart and tail

As the liquid mixture heats up, the substances with the lowest boiling point vaporise. For vinaccia, those substances that vaporise would be acetaldehyde, acetic acid, ethyl acetate and the poisonous methyl alcohol (methanol). This initial vapour is called the distillate's *testa* (head) and is separated out from the process by the distiller.

Between 78°C and 100°C the ethyl alcohol, the aroma and the best of the flavour are released from the raw material – as well as water. This part of the distillate is called the *cuore* (heart). It is this that will become the finished grappa.

At temperatures above 100°C the remaining liquid begins to vaporise – these are the most viscose elements of the vinaccia containing higher alcohols, also known as fusel oils. They are called "oils" because they can be seen with the naked eye. Examples of these oils include propanol, butanol and amyl alcohol. These make up the *coda* (tail) that is also separated away.

Pressure and temperature

The temperature of the steam is decisive for the quality of the grappa. There is a causal relation between steam pressure and temperature: the higher the pressure, the higher the temperature. When making grappa, the steam temperature should be high enough to release the sought-after aromas from the grape skins, but not too high that the seeds release their bitter oil. Less careful industries use steam pressures of around 1 atmosphere (atm) or more which generates temperatures up to 100 - 115°C. Smaller distilleries often work with less pressure – below 1 atm, resulting in lower steam temperatures of around 102 - 105°C. This allows a more gentle treatment of the raw material.

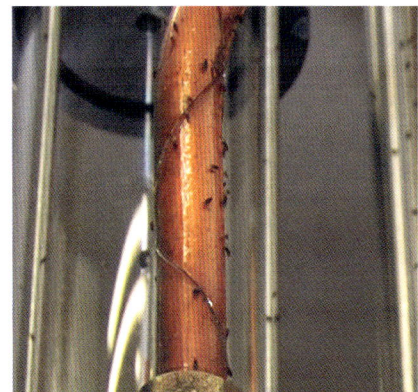

Moscerini, the tiny flies present in all distilleries, love vinaccia and descend on the grappa if so much as a single drop finds its way outside the alambicco. Some even claim that they prefer cuore. Well – millions of moscerini cannot be wrong!

Winning the heart of grappa

It is during the separation of the *cuore* that the *maestro* shows their skill. It is here that they can display their passion, love and craftsmanship. By mastering the distilling technique and *alambicco* they become less and less reliant on the equipment. Boilers, pipes and valves are affected by use, wear and tear or faulty parts; however, it does not really matter, because in the hands of a master a quality raw product will produce a quality grappa.

There are as many ways to capture the *cuore* as there are distillers. Some look objectively at the alcohol strength as an automatic release mechanism for the *cuore*. Others believe that the *cuore* is brought out only through a distiller's sense of smell and taste as developed after years of training. It has to do with how to separate substances that can distort or damage the grappa. The poisonous methanol though has neither taste or odour.

Regardless, it is the alcohol meter that is a distiller's most reliable tool. Whichever method they use, they always keep one eye on the buoyant alcohol meter inside the glass cover.

Grappa is a compromise

Distillation has two steps: first in the boiler where the substances are released as a vapour from the vinaccia, and then in the distillation column where the alcohol condenses and the aroma is gradually concentrated. At the outset, vinaccia has an alcohol content of around 4-6 percent. After leaving the vinaccia, the vapour has an alcohol content of around 20-25 percent. This *flemma* is led into the base of the distillation column and is reheated. As the steam rises the alcohol content increases step by step.

The vapour that has managed to make its way through the entire length of the distillation column is then cooled to form a liquid. The first liquid, the *testa*, contains the easily evaporated substances. This is siphoned off or returned to the distillation column to go through the process again. The distillate's alcohol strength steadily increases and when it reaches the boiling point for ethanol (78.4°C) the distiller switches the flow to capture it. This is the *cuore* – the actual grappa. The distiller then lets the flow continue until the grappa nears 60-65 percent alcohol. At this point the flow from the still becomes *coda* and the distiller switches the flow again to separate it.

The exact timing of siphoning off the *cuore* varies from distiller to distiller. From an aroma and taste point of view, there are sought-after elements in both the *testa* and the *coda*, just as there are unwanted flavours in the *cuore*. It is not so simple that all substances can be separated step by step along the way. One can say that they are all present at all times.

To capture the *cuore* is the art of compromise.

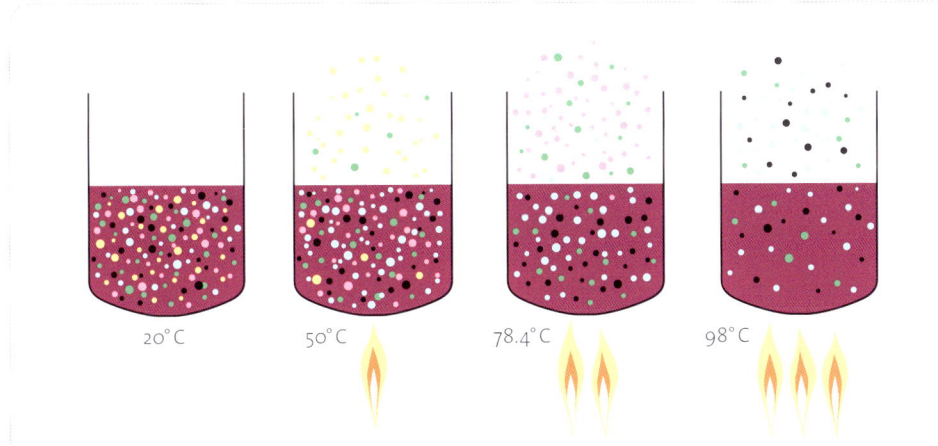

The picture illustrates the grounding principles of distilling: how various substances and elements can be drawn out of the raw material at differing temperatures. Note that desirable aromas can be found in all the categories, which means that only certain aromas end up in the final product.

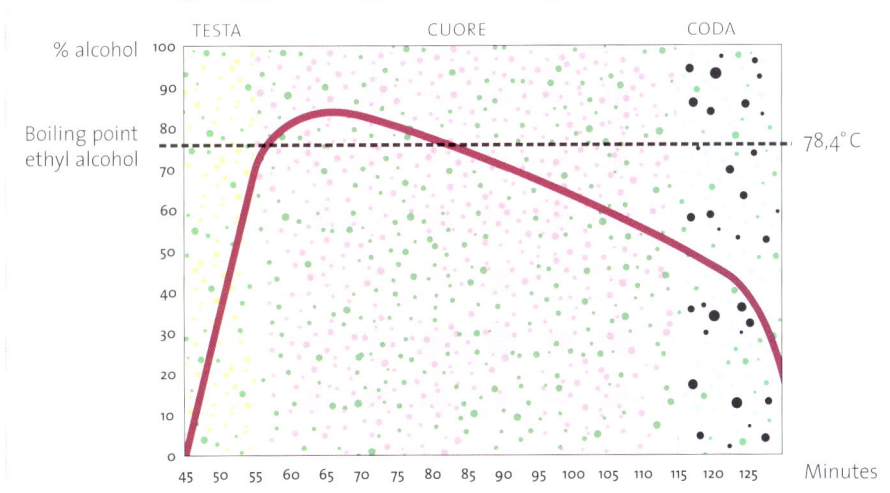

The profile shows the development of alcohol content that occurs during distillation and how at certain levels the distiller can separate the testa, cuore and coda. The picture also demonstrates the dilemma of the distiller – which desirable aromas will be left out since they keep coming all the time.

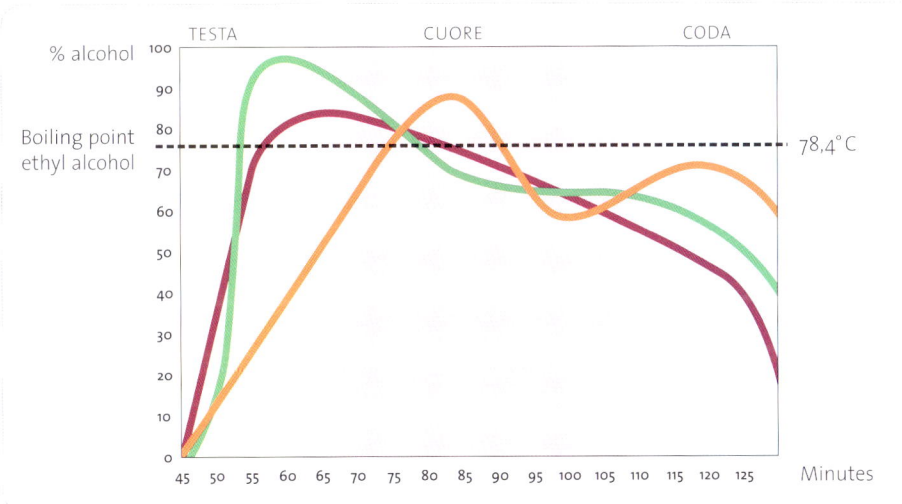

Every grappa has its own profile. The difference is due to the grape variety's characteristics and as well as the distiller's skill, taste and intentions.

Types of boilers

Boiler for boutique batchwise production *a bagnomaria*.

Boiler for boutique batchwise production *a vapore diretto*.

Boiler for industrial production *a continuo*.

2. Colonna di distillazione – the column condenses the aroma and alcohol into a concentrate.

Coperchio – the lid also called *duomo* (dome) *capitello* (capital), *capello* (hat), *elmo* (helmet). The vapour gathers in the top where the first condensation occurs – when part of the steam is cooled against the walls of the dome and forms a liquid which drops down again. Other vapours continue upwards.

Collo di cigno – the swan's neck, the name of a crocked pipe.

80% alcohol – 20% water

1. Caldaia – heated boiler, also called *paiolo* (copper bell) *cucurbita* (curbits, pump). This is where the vinaccia is heated and the substances within the vinaccia boil and become vapour.

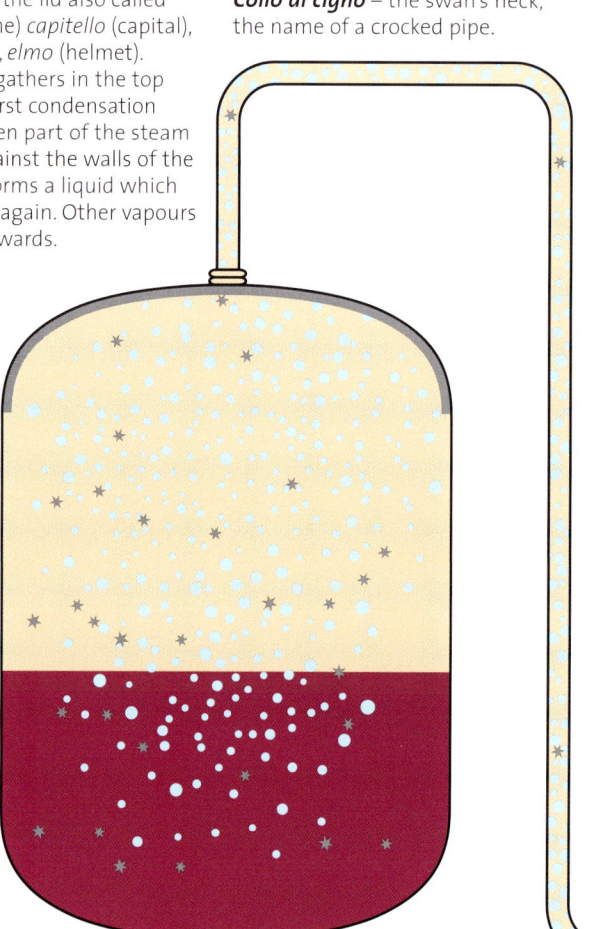

Vinaccia 600 litres
5% alcohol – 95% water

20% alcohol – 80% water
(flemma)

Alcohol and aroma substances

Non-desirable substances

ALAMBICCO – THE STILL

A still is a relatively simple construction, which in its most basic form is made up of six parts:
1. Boiler. 2. Distilling column. 3. Cooling tank. 4. Alcohol meter gauge. 5. Volume gauge. 6. Collection container.
The illustration shows the principle of a traditional method for batchwise distilling – *discontinuo a bagnomaria*.

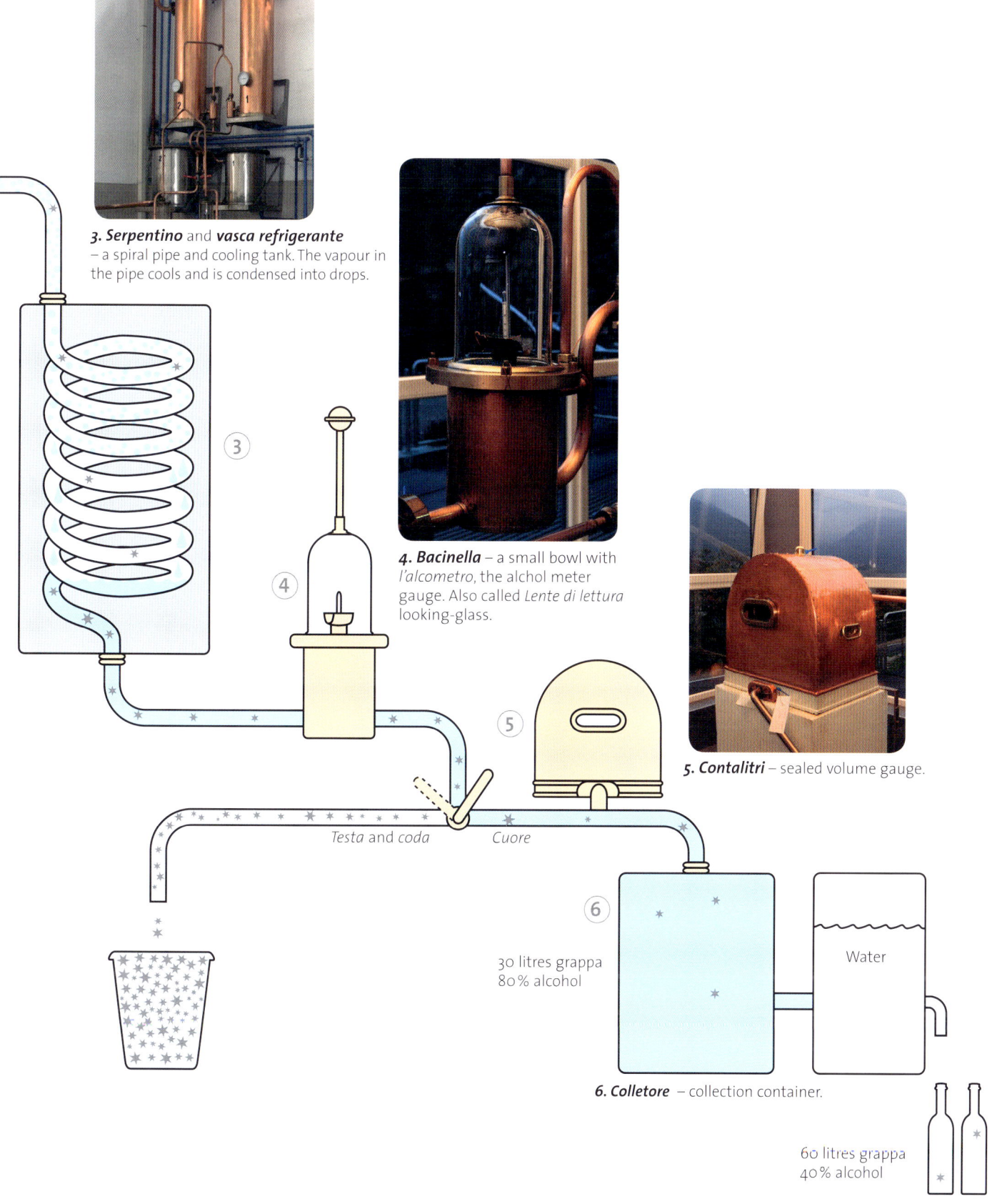

3. Serpentino and ***vasca refrigerante***
– a spiral pipe and cooling tank. The vapour in the pipe cools and is condensed into drops.

4. Bacinella – a small bowl with *l'alcometro*, the alchol meter gauge. Also called *Lente di lettura* looking-glass.

5. Contalitri – sealed volume gauge.

Testa and *coda*   *Cuore*

30 litres grappa
80% alcohol

Water

6. Colletore – collection container.

60 litres grappa
40% alcohol

Distillation column

In the distillation column the precious vapour rises: alcohol and aroma substances concentrate more and more while water and the heavier elements fall back. As the alcohol content increases, also aroma substances and tiny impurities decrease which can be interesting from a taste point of view. However, through the column a master distiller can shape the grappa characteristics by fine-tuning the process.

Within the column there are plates that let through and condense the vapour. The more plates, the more effective the distillation process is. However, it also reduces the aroma along the way. In principle, the better and fresher the vinaccia is, the fewer plates are required. Some small boutique distillers have columns with only three plates – others have up to ten or more.

Rectification column

Industrial distilleries do not have the same possibilities as small boutique distilleries to personalise their grappa. This is mainly due to the raw product as their vinaccia has been stored for a long time and undergone changes that demand more rigorous distilling and cleaning processes. Rectification is only seen in large industrial grappa production and essentially it means that the grappa is distilled, one more time, in a particularly tall distillation column. The result is a chemically clean grappa high in alcohol – but with less aroma and taste profile.

Every plate in the column can be viewed as a single distillation step. The plates have holes which allow the vapour to go through and condense in the mushroom-shaped hat. Heavier substances like water and alcohol are collected on the plate and heated once again, the vapour rises and moves on to the next plate etc. When the liquid on a plate reaches a certain level it trickles back down the bent pipe in the column and the plate below.

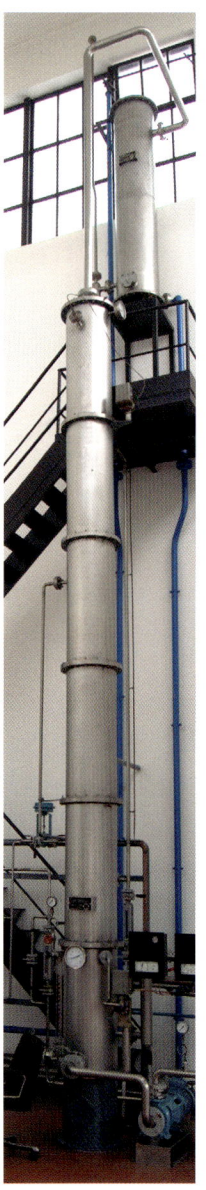

DISTILLATION METHODS

CONTINUOUS DISTILLATION
DISTILLAZIONE A CONTINUA

The industrial distillers use continuous distillation: the raw product is added, distilled and removed from the still in an automated process without cessation. Distilleries began using this technique in the 60's and 70's to increase production and reduce their costs. The principle of continuous distillation was discovered by F.lli Stemmer in 1877 who constructed a grappa boiler where vinaccia was placed in cupboard-like baskets. When the vinaccia in the lowest basket was exhausted it was removed and a new basket was simultaneously introduced at the top. In this way the raw product moved downwards, was used and gradually expelled without production needing to halt.

In this distilling process (which can be either horizontally or vertically constructed) the vinaccia is fed from one direction where it is met by steam that takes up the alcohol and aromatic substances. This method makes it possible to get maximum benefit from the raw material, i.e. greatest possible volume of grappa. The drawback of this method, from a taste perspective, is that large scale production requires vinaccia in volumes that make it almost impossible to be selective with the raw material. However, the grappa has a consistently even character and quality that is important to big companies and brands; their customers want to be certain about what they are getting.

80 percent of all grappa is produced using continuous distillation techniques. These companies represent about 30 percent of the total number of distilleries.

Capacity: 100-200 tonnes of vinaccia every day.

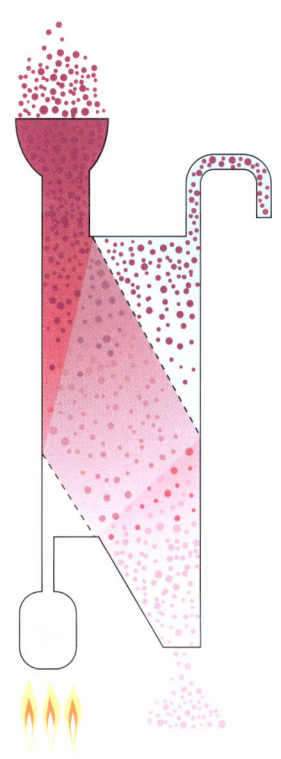

BATCHWISE OR DIS-CONTINUOUS DISTILLATION
DISTILLAZIONE A DISCONTINUA

The smaller boutique distilleries use a dis-continuous distillation process – one batch at a time. The boiler is loaded with a batch of vinaccia that is distilled by hand, the boiler is then emptied, cleaned and reloaded with a new batch. The advantage, from a taste perspective, is that it is possible to distil fresh vinaccia of various grapes and amounts. Thanks to the long extraction process of aromatic and other substances, it is possible to regulate the temperature and length of the process to affect the character of the grappa. The disadvantage is that it is cumbersome to handle and process the fresh vinaccia, not to mention as cleaning the boiler after each use *(cotta)*.

There are three batchwise methods: *a bagnomaria, a vapore diretto* and *a fuoco diretto*. The difference is in how they heat the vinaccia in the boiler to produce the vapours.

Distillazione a bagnomaria

Bagnomaria literally means water bath – double-boiling is a common cooking technique to gently heat the content of the upper pot using the steam from the hot water in the lower pot.

This is the softest, most gentle method of all and therefore the least effective, i.e. it gives the lowest alcohol exchange or return on the volume of vinaccia.

The boiler of an *alambicco a bagnomaria* is covered by an outer boiler. The "inner boiler" is filled with vinaccia and water and the heat is applied from the "outer boiler" being filled with steam or hot water that is generated separately. This indirect heat creates a soft, gentle steam from the vinaccia.

This is the oldest method still in use today on a larger scale, especially in Trentino and Piemonte. In the 1950's and 60's Tullio Zadra from Trentino refined the technique by introducing new gauges and copper boilers.

Today, there are around 40 distilleries with *alambicchi a bagnomaria* – or approximately a third of all distilleries – and are responsible for about 5 percent of the total production of grappa.

Capacity: One batch of 1200 litres (600 kg (1300 lb) vinaccia + water) takes 5-6 hours.

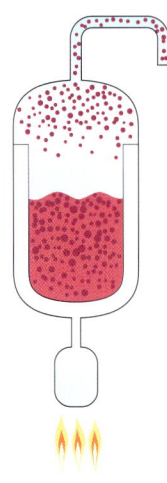

Distillazione a vapore diretto

With this method, the vinaccia is not blended with water but instead is placed dry in a basket inside the boiler. *Vapore* or steam is generated separately and pumped into the boiler from underneath. The steam this heats the raw material and extracts the alcohol and aromatic substances. This method was developed in the 1800s to improve quality and increase productivity. At that time, however, water was put in the bottom of the boiler and directly heated to create steam.

Today, *distillazione a vapore diretto* is the classic method used by boutique distillers and craftsmen. It is used by approximately 60 distilleries, especially in Veneto, Friuli, Lombardia and also Piemonte, and accounts for approximately 15 percent of the total grappa produced in Italy.

Capacity: A boiler containing 200-600kg (440-1320 lb) of vinaccia takes between 1 to 3 hours to distil.

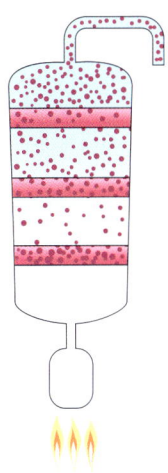

Distillazione a fuoco diretto

Distillation with heat applied *directly* through fire to the boiler. It is the oldest method of distilling and is in principle no longer used in commercial distilling, but rather so to demonstrate a tradition. However a few distilleries still use *fuoco diretto*.

Vinaccia and water are put into the boiler which is heated over an open wood fire, gas flame or fire of the used vinaccia. The process demands intense scrutiny so that the vinaccia will not burn and transfer a burnt flavour to the grappa. This risk is the main reason for the development of the more gentle methods of *bagnomaria* and *vapore diretto*.

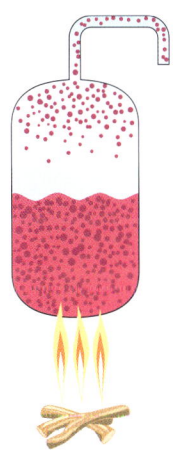

Dilution and ageing

Grappa from the *alambicco* is crystal clear with a quality and aromatic profile that reflects the grapes and the raw material's handling before and during distillation. Unlike many other alcoholic beverages that are born without any aromatic potential, grappa really does not need additional aroma or to be aged in oak barrels. After distillation, it only needs to be diluted with water and allowed to rest for six months. Then it is ready to enjoy. All grappa, and all other distillates, are born white as pigmentation cannot be distilled. Coloured spirits gets their nuances from ageing in oak barrels or through food colouring.

Grappa direct from the *alambicco* has an alcohol content of around 70-86 percent. At this level there is still aroma lingering. Generally, the higher the alcohol content, the more defects – and desirable flavours – are separated out from the distillate.

Lowering the alcohol content

The grappa from the still is diluted with water until it is has a consumable alcohol strength of between 40-60 percent. The quality of the water is important – it should be colourless, odourless and flavourless, plus it should not contain lime or magnesium which can cause sediment to form. Most commonly used to dilute grappa is distilled or treated water. In rare cases, distilleries source the water from pure springs.

Regardless of the compounds in the water, it reacts with the grappa during dilution. The temperature rises, the volume decreases slightly and the mixture becomes half-transparent or a touch milky. Chilling the grappa to between minus 10-20°C causes sediment to form which can then be easily filtered away. This "sediment" is actually salts, acids and fusel oils; unfortunately some of the pleasant aroma can also get caught up in this filtration process.

Ageing

Many believe that grappa direct from the still is perfect; it already has its aroma and only needs a six month resting period after the shock-treatment in the *alambicco*.

To produce grappa that has additional aroma and colour, it must be aged in oak barrels. Ageing *(invecchiamento)* is still debated amongst grappa experts, as the wood alters the original sensory profile. Regardless, almost all the distilleries have oak-aged grappa in their stock. Ageing is an effective way to create new flavours and develop new products.

With ageing comes grappa's *lungo sonno* (long sleep), where even the temperature and humidity in the store room contribute to the final result. Longer-time ageing takes place in giant vats that hold around 10-15,000 litres or in a smaller vats – *barrique* – for shorter ageing periods. Oak, mostly Slovenian oak, is the dominant wood, however barrels made of wood from ash, juniper, cherry, almond, melon, apple, pear and so on can be used. Still, critics warn of the risk of changing the grappa without improving it.

During ageing, the grappa develops in two ways: *extraction* and *oxidisation*. *Extraction* is the leaking of the aromatic properties of the wood and the tannins into the grappa. This is essential when ageing in smaller barrels. For example, in new *barriques* a grappa can be stored for just a few weeks – longer and it becomes bitter and undrinkable.

Oxidisation happens when storing grappa in larger vats for longer periods: the porous wooden walls of the barrel allow some air through, which reacts with the grappa and forms esters (aromas). That air can enter the vat also means that a certain quantity of the grappa evaporates during cellaring.

Grappa is aged both undiluted and diluted, mostly undiluted.

Grappa by definition

Grappa is an Italian distillate of grape solids (vinaccia). The term grappa is protected by EU Regulation No. 1576/89 and cannot be used outside of Italy, except for Canton Ticino in Switzerland. How grappa is distilled, and most importantly the requirement of grape solids, is regulated by the Italian Government through the Decree 297/97. For example, one requirement is that the grapes must be grown and processed in Italy.

No distillery outside of Italy can distil vinaccia and call the drink grappa. Instead they can call it "acquavite from vinaccia", "vinaccia distillate" or something to that effect on the label. The equivalent of grappa in Germany is called *Tresterbrand*, in France they say *marc* and in Spain *orujo*.

Grappa is a unique distillate because it is produced from a non-liquid raw material containing an unusually large concentration of aromatic substances. Whereas brandy and similar distillates contain only the secondary aromas of the grape (wine aromas), the vinaccia adds primary aromas of the grape to the grappa.

This does not mean that grappa in general has a richer taste than other distillates, since the aroma also depend on how the raw material is distilled. However, gas chromatography tests show that grappa can contain almost twice as many aroma substances as brandy. Of course our tasting sensory organs can only perceive a few of them.

Alcohol strength
The alcoholic content of the grappa from the *alambicco* must not exceed 86 percent (percentage by volume). All grappa must be diluted with water to a consumer strength of between 60 and 37.5 percent. The original strength of grappa also varies but if it is not too high it can be bottled undiluted as full proof *pieno grado*. If a distillate is over 86 percent it cannot be called grappa but instead is called a *spirit*. At these levels there is quite simply no aroma or flavour left.

Classified grappa with designation of origin from Barolo, Piemonte, Lombardia, Alto Adige, Trentino, Veneto and Friuli must not have an alcoholic strength of less than 40 percent. Furthermore, the grapes must have a proof of origin.

Other additives
Besides water, the distillery is allowed to add 2 percent sugar and 3 percent natural additives such as herb, fruit, aromas or natural colouring (caramel colour i.e. burnt sugar) per litre undiluted grappa. The regulations require that these additives do not affect the grappa's genuine sensory profile. However, none of these additives has to be stated on the label. For example, it is acceptable to add colour to grappa that has been stored in oak barrels in order to increase the aged look. A grappa "Chardonnay" may contain sugar as well as natural colouring and natural aromatic additives.

The grappa industry in general is trying to find ways to get rid of the 3 percentage rule. Boutique distillers never use substances of this kind.

Sugar – a burning issue
The use of sugar is debated amongst distillers and aficionados. The argument goes to the soul of grappa. How should grappa really taste? Fierce anti-sugar purists believe that sugar changes the genuine character of grappa and should be forbidden. Others think that sugar in small quantities is needed to round out a grappa made from over-pressed vinaccia or from less aromatic grape varieties, or of course when the vinaccia is poorly stored. *Note*: Sugar in the grapes cannot be transferred into the grappa via distillation. But a grappa still can have a sweet scent without the presence of sugar.

Flavoured grappa

Herbs, berries and fruits are the oldest colouring and aromatic additives for food. Grappa can also be spiced and perfumed with a whole range of herbs and spices such as camomile, mint, sage, honeysuckle, wormwood, juniper, blueberries, nettles, coffee and so on. These grappas are called *grappa aromatizzata* and are not subject to the 3-percent rule when it comes to the amount of allowed natural substances. However, the label must show that it is a grappa *aromatizzata*. As the perfuming of grappa dramatically changes its character, this kind of flavoured grappa falls into a different category and therefore also outside of the scope of this book.

Aged grappa

To be able to call a grappa *vecchia* or *invecchiata* (aged), it must be cellared for at least 12 months in wooden barrels. The terms *riserva* or *stravecchia* (extra-aged) mean the grappa has been aged for at least 18 months in wooden barrels.

Gold with a shimmer of mystique

An alambicco is built of copper and stainless steel. Copper has characteristics that are essential to a distiller. This metal is a good conductor of heat, an important factor in this high energy-consuming process. According to distillers, copper also has the ability to integrate – a concept they sometimes have a hard time explaining. Some talk about copper's ability to act as a catalyst when breaking down unwanted substances and in this way contributing to the quality of the grappa. Generally, copper is used in parts of the still where there is a higher alcohol content and steel is used where the alcohol content is lower. The liquids with lower alcohol content can cause oxidation and release copper oxide into the grappa.

What is in a grappa

Grappa primarily consist of almost equal mixtures of water and ethyl alcohol. This blend – which is completely tasteless – makes up 99 percent of the grappa content. The elements that give it aroma and flavour make up only about 1 percent of the total volume. It is these small impurities – these "defects" – that make grappa a unique sensory experience. These "defects" include esters, aldehydes, terpenes and organic acids. If it had been distilled "perfectly", the grappa would have been free from all aroma and flavour.

Water
The water comes from the diluting of the final product but also from the vinaccia and steam from the distillation process.

Alcohol
In the grappa there are alcohols or specifically: ethanol, methanol and some higher alcohols such as fusel oils.

Ethanol or *ethyl alcohol* is the most important alcohol in the grappa. Ethanol is a colourless liquid with a pleasant smell, fiery taste and inebriating effect. Ethanol can be mixed with water to any proportions and is a solvent for many substances. This is important for the dilution of a grappa, the aroma and the ageing characteristics.

Methanol or *methyl alcohol* is a highly poisonous and wily alcohol as it is colourless, flavourless and odourless. Methanol – distiller's enemy number one – is found in vinaccia that is stored incorrectly or for longer periods. According to the laws governing grappa, it can contain at the most 1 ml of methanol per 100 ml of undiluted grappa.

Higher alcohols are aroma substances that are significant to a grappa – in good and bad ways. These alcohols occur during fermentation and preserving of vinaccia – and also form fusel oils. Higher alcohols can often have a more inebriating effect than ethanol but are present in such small quantities that it makes no real difference.

Some examples include propanol, butanol, isopropanol, isobutanol, isoamyl alcohol.

Esters
Nature is full of esters. They give flowers and fruits their perfume and flavour. Esters are the product of a chemical reaction between carboxylic acid and alcohol. The most important ester for grappa is ethyl acetate (i.e. acetic acid + ethanol) which has a strong and fruity but pungent smell. Other examples of fruity esters include ethyl lactate, ethyl propionate, ethyl caprylate, isoamyl acetate and isobutyl acetate. In high concentrations, esters can cause a sour flavour.

Aldehydes
Aldehydes are natural, aromatic substances that occur when alcohol oxidises. These are aroma-rich even in small quantities. Acetaldehyde is the most common aldehyde in grappa and in the right quantities gives a pleasant, fruity aroma. Aldehydes are not always pleasant in odour - butyr aldehyde has a pungent odour and furfural, which can be produced if the vinaccia is incorrectly heated, gives grappa a burnt taste.

Terpenes
Terpenes are strongly aromatic substances that are present in all essential oils. These are made up of long carbon and hydrogen chains with amazing structures. Citronellol is a characteristic terpene with a fragrance of roses and citrus fruits. It can be found in grappa made from aromatic grapes such as Muscat, Gewürztraminer and Riesling.

Organic acids
Good grappa is not acidic, but acids are significant for a grappa's personality because acids create esters together with alcohol. Common acids in grappa include acetic acid, propionic acid, butyric acid, isovaleria acid, pelargonic acid, capronic acid, caprylic acid and lactic acid.

Classification and grappa varieties

Division by distilling method

Grappa discontinuo
- Boutique grappas. Strong in alcohol with rich aromas and tastes, made in a traditional manner by smaller distilleries.

Grappa continuo
- Mass produced grappas. More neutral in aromas and tastes than grappa *discontinuo*. Represents the majority of the grappa on the market.

Division by age and grape

Grappa giovane or *grappa bianca*
- *Young or white* grappa aged in glass or steel containers for at least 6 months.
- The grappa is crystal clear with aromas solely from the grapes and fermentation.

Grappa affinata in legno
- Grappa aged in wooden barrels for 6-12 months.
- The finished grappa has received its colour and flavour from the ageing process.

Grappa invecchiata
- Grappa called *vecchia* or *invecchiata* is aged wooden vats for at least 12 months. To be called *riserva* or *stravecchia* it must be aged for at least 18 months.
- The finished grappa's colour, sensory profile and character is strongly affected by the ageing process.

Grappa aromatica
- All the groups above can be given the term *aromatica* – for example, *grappa giovane aromatica*, *grappa affinata in legno aromatica* or *grappa invecchiata aromatica*
- This term means that the grappa is made from *vinaccia* from aromatic grape varieties such as Muscat, Gewurtztraminer or half-aromatic varieties like Müller-Thurgau, Prosecco or Sauvignon Blanc.
- For the aged grappa, *aromatica* signals that the grape's original character is still noticeable.

Grappa aromatizzata
- Grappa whose sensory profile is essentially changed through spicing with herbs, roots and other natural additives, commonly with a naturopathic purpose.

Grappa monovitigno, univitigno or *di vitigno*
- This classification can be used for grappa where at least 85 percent of its contents has been distilled from vinaccia from a single grape variety – *vitigno* – which is shown on the label. The concept has in recent years increasingly come into use also for *winery grappa** and grappa produced from *vinaccia* from renowned wines and thereby changing the original meaning of *monovitigno*. Recognize that the fact that a grappa has the same name as a famous wine is no guarantee of its quality or flavour.

Division by geographic origin

This category is reserved for grappa that is made from grapes that are grown, harvested and vinificated in certain regions. The alcohol content must be at least 40 percent. This includes:

- *grappa di Barolo*
- *grappa piemontese* or *del Piemonte*
- *grappa lombarda* or *della Lombardia*
- *grappa trentina* or *del Trentino*
- *grappa dell´Alto Adige* or *Südtiroler Grappa*
- *grappa veneta* or *del Veneto*
- *grappa friulana* or *del Friuli*

* *Winery grappa* is a relatively new phenomenon with its origin in Tuscany. A winery grappa is made at a distillery by order of a wine maker who delivers the vinaccia from a single wine brand. This brand will also end up denoting the grappa, for example Grappa di Brunello di Montalcino. Whereas *grappa monovitigno* can, in principle, be produced from grapes from anywhere in Italy, the vinaccia for winery grappa must originate from the wine district or vineyard stated on the label. A winery grappa belong to the winery's assortment of offerings, not the distillery's.

Wine tasting

Wine does not taste or smell like grapes – it tastes and smells like an orchard. When you merely drink a wine you experience the flavour. By tasting a wine you experience its entirety – the sum of the aroma, taste on the tongue, persistence of flavour and colour. When tasting a wine the bouquet is the most important, then the taste and last and the colour. However, a wine must always be viewed in its entirety; the harmony that is created between all the sensory impressions.

Appearance
A wine's appearance – *the first of the sensory impressions* – reveals any impurities that might require a wine to be decanted. According to connoisseurs, a wine's consistency, as well as nuance and intensity of colour, gives away the age and quality of a wine. For a novice, it is difficult to judge a wine's appearance.

Bouquet
The aromas are a result of chemical substances and reactions in the wine. To release a wine's aroma the wine is agitated with a vigorous swirling action. Then the nose is thrust into the bell of the glass and the aroma is breathed in through the nose in a slow, deep inhalation. This *nasal* tasting provides *the second sensory impression* and can expose any imperfections and also gives wine connoisseurs a clue to the grape variety used in the wine, its origin and location.

The aromas
The simplest chemical reaction occur first. For white wines these cause fruity aromas reminiscent of banana, melons, apple, peach etc. For red wines the aroma is often likened to red berries, cherries and plums. Then the floral aromas such as flower, leaves and grass become apparent.

Simpler wines reflect only the aroma of the grapes – which is more than adequate – but then we are not really talking about a *bouquet* of aromas. Bouquet refers to even those perfumes and smells that are specific to a wine's *terroir*, vintage and method of production. With white wines it can have an association of honey, hay, butter cake, vanilla, cedar and minerals. And red wines also refer to spicy overtones, chocolate, coffee, smoke and woody tones.

Nuances of the unusual, such as a hint of sauerkraut, soap, vinegar, wet wool and petrol can positively enhance a wine's bouquet.

Palate
The taste, or palate of a wine – *the third sensory impression* – reveals the balance between sweet and sour and with red wines unveils the tannin content, as well as consistency, the quality of the after-taste or persistence and alcohol content. As a general rule, the higher the alcohol content, the rounder a wine becomes.

The balance between sweetness and acidity is decisive for a white wine. The acidity provides freshness and crispness, but too much can make a wine bitter and too little makes it flat or dull. Simpler wines are often more acidic due to harvesting of unripe grapes. Sweetness in the wine demands equilibrium in the form of fruit acid and bitterness from wooden barrels.

Red wine's main difference in flavour from white wine is due to the presence of tannin – tannic acid – which exists in both grape skins and oak barrels. The tannins, which are bitter, harsh and have an astringent effect, are a vital component of all great wines. It is all about the balance between sweetness, acidity and bitterness.

Persistence or length
The taste buds on the tongue can discern only the basic flavours: sweet, sour, bitter, salt and umami. The rich nuances are experienced *retro-nasally* via aromas which resonate with the olfactory senses from the back of the mouth and up into the nose.

The critical and decisive moment for the judging of a wine is the consumption – what happens?

A great wine fills the mouth and throat, the wine will provide a rich *retro-nasal* experience with aromas of fruity berries, caramel, woods and coffee – that also linger and persist. Wines which only confirm the tongue's first impression and then dissipate quickly after swallowing are called "short".

The fruits of the Caco tree.

Grappa tasting

Compared to the number of available wines there are few grappas and outside of Italy there are far fewer. And if you are looking for boutique grappas you are unlikely to have many options – if you can find any at all. To find a selection to taste you will probably have to look for well-stocked restaurants or source a grappa specialist.

Grappa is tasted differently from wine because grappa is a different and much stronger drink with a different purpose. Wine tasting is performed on certain occasions or moments – for example when a new bottle is opened or when a glass of wine is served – and afterwards the wine is enjoyed. A grappa on the other hand should be tasted *every time!* At *every* intake of the bouquet, at *each* mouthful, at *every* swallow and at *every* taste sensation and association.

Grappa is a complex sensory experience that simulates an inner-dialogue as well as a discussion around the table.

Speak your mind
A grappa has a spectrum, or as the Italians say *ventaglio* (folding fan), of aromas that can be investigated and analysed to various degrees. It is enough to just smell and drink the grappa to set off associations and quietly enjoy the images, feelings, memories or whatever turns up on your inner journey. You can also use a more methodical approach, as wine tasters do, and perform a sensory analysis – even if the result is a highly personal judgement. Regardless of the weight of such an analysis it is interesting to know how our instruments work: our senses – sight, smell, taste and touch. The more you use your abilities to recognise the nose and palate that have meaning for you, the richer the experience will be. That is not equal to be able to put terms on every association. The palate is complex and above all, fleeting – and sometimes cannot be captured in a word or two. However, in discussing your experience with others you do not have much to use but words.

Grappa and stress do not mix
Does not the high alcoholic strength make tasting difficult? Alcohol is responsible for creating the aroma in grappa, but it is not necessary for your tasting experience. It is possible to sense the quality of the aroma without consuming a grappa. If you do not want to taste it – tip a few drops into the palm of your hand and rub your hands together, then cup your hands to collect the *fan* of aromas and inhale deeply through your nose. This is a common practise of many grappa makers.

You can also dilute the grappa with a little warm water or inhale the aroma from an emptied glass. Some grappa masters believe that the best time for tasting a grappa is early in the morning before consuming any food as the taste buds are at their most sensitive. They of course view it more professionally! Whichever way you choose, it is advisable to let the grappa rest a while before tasting. Some varieties of grappa change dramatically once they are in the glass.

Temperature for consumption
Grappa giovane, not too cold: 10-15°C
Grappa invecchiata, room temperature 17-20°C

Type of glass
Some prefer cognac glasses, others prefer wine tasting glasses and many choose the "typical" grappa glass. These are often designed and marketed by certain grappa producers and therefore, in Italy, are closely associated with a particular label. Take your pick.

Tasting sequence
1. Grappa giovane
2. Grappa invecchiata
3. Grappa giovane aromatica
4. Grappa invecchiata aromatica

APPEARANCE

1. A GRAPPA'S LOOK

Grappa is judged in part on its clarity or colour. All grappa is at first white. Distillation is a cleaning process and *grappa giovane* should be transparent and sparkle like crystal. If not, then the grappa was poorly distilled, filtered or aged. Lime in the water used to dilute a grappa can create a natural sediment that disappears during filtration. Colour changes towards yellow or blue are a sign of iron or copper from the *alambicco* – defects that the distiller should correct with a second distillation and cleansing.

Barrel aged *grappa invecchiata* has colours from hay yellow to deep amber. If the grappa is stored in big barrels that have been used for long, they can get little, if any, colour from the wood. This may also indicate that some important flavours are missing. On the other hand caramel colouring – produced by heating sugar – can be added to enhance the impression of an "aged" grappa.

BOUQUET

2. THE AROMA OF GRAPPA

The nose is our most important tasting sensory organ! The olfactory sense is hypersensitive and equipped with a good memory. Surprising aromas can allow us to momentarily travel in time. Normally, we are not required to analyse aromas; our instincts tell us if something is good or bad – if it is edible or not.

When analysing an aroma one problem is our fast adaptation. We experience it as if the smell dissipates after only 4 or 5 seconds. That is because our olfactory senses are constantly resetting to enable us to register new odours and aromas in our surroundings. Naturally, flowers, wine or grappa exude scents all the time, but we have just a moment to identify an aroma and put it into words. This is when a wine taster's well-trained nose, sure associations and personal vocabulary come into use, as our olfactory sense is believed to register around 400,000 different scents.

Wine and grappa aromas reach the mucous membranes of the nose in two stages. First when it is breathed in via the nose – *nasal* – and again when we swallow and the aroma reaches our nose via the nasal passages at the back of our throat – *retro-nasal*. The aromas alter slightly as saliva, our breath and the warmth of our mouth all affect a liquid's volatile substances.

Primary, secondary and tertiary aromas
Professionals talk about *primary aromas* when they taste *grappa giovane* to describe how the grape of origin – often aromatic or half-aromatic – affects the grappa's character. *Secondary aromas* are produced during the fermentation and can include alcohols, acids, esters, aldehydes and other substances. Secondary aromas can also form during distillation and often give a pleasant hint of liquorice. *Tertiary aromas* belong to *grappa invecchiata* and spring from the ageing in wooden barrels. (*Quartary aromas* occur with *grappa aromatizzata*).

A brandy for example contain no primary aromas, since it is distilled from wine and not the grape(skins).

Fragance and odour
An aroma that is not normally associated with food and beverage can be the sign that really makes a wine or a grappa. That the aroma is unusual is not a barrier but a boon. But it is another thing entirely if it smells bad, an odour that is off – that is a warning signal, a stop sign! A grappa's quality is increased by the quantity of pleasant aromas and the absence of any undesirable odours.

Pleasant aromas

Grass
This aroma is caused primarily by acetate aldehyde and unsaturated aldehydes which are formed during the storage of vinaccia. It is pleasant in small amounts.

Melon, banana, strawberries...and exotic fruits
A really lovely fruity sensation created by the presence of various esters.

Nuts
The nutty aroma comes from an alcohol that is formed when the poly-saturated fatty acids found in vinaccia, like linolic acid and linoleic acid, are broken down.

Hyacinth
A pleasant flowery smell stemming from the presence of phenyl acetate aldehyde.

Peaches
This perfume is created in a grappa as a result of extremely fresh and pure vinaccia. It is caused by esters and lactones.

Raspberries
This is a slightly strange sensation found in fruity grappas. It is caused by phenyl esters such as ethyl cinnamate and ethyl lactate.

Lily of the Valley, lilies and nutmeg
This is a classic and easily identified aroma commonly found in grappa from aromatic grape varieties. It is caused by various aromatic substances within the terpene family.

Rose
A very special and surprising perfume in grappa made from Müller-Thurgau grapes and caused by phenethyl acetate.

FLAVOUR

3. THE TASTE OF GRAPPA

The capacity of a palate is somewhat over-estimated. To discuss a dish's, a wine's or a grappa's outstanding taste is misplaced. Our taste buds can only differentiate between the five basic flavours – sweet, sour, salt, bitter and umami. Umami is the Japanese word for delicious – it is a metallic taste that exists in vegetables, cheese, soya, shellfish and meat. That we can experience a "flavour" is thanks to our subtle sense of smell. Even the texture plays a role in how we taste, as does the appearance. "Flavour" is more of a holistic experience based on the sum of how our senses reacts.

When talking about flavour it is common to refer to where on the tongue a flavour is sensed. Sweet on the tip of the tongue, bitter is at the back and so on. Nowadays, it is believed that flavour is too complex to be localised to particular parts of the tongue. The basic flavours are experienced by the whole tongue.

With alcohol our sense of taste plays a minor role – and for an alcoholic drink as strong as grappa it has even less weight. Alcohol has a tendency to dry out the mucus membrane but just as quickly a warmth spreads, then a certain softness and at last the flavour. In comparison with wine, grappa has little flavour – only two: sweet and bitter. Pure distillate has little body by definition – the more a liquid is distilled, the greater the flavour and flavour substances, are separated away.

Sweet
Sweet flavours together with bitter flavours contribute to the rounding out of the burning effects of the alcohol. Sweet and bitter provides a certain harmony, balance and body to a grappa. Pure, white *grappa giovane* contains no sugar. The sweetness in grappa comes from added sugar or from the barrel if it is aged *invecchiata*. Grappa without sweetness is called dry *secco*.

Bitter
Bitterness balanced with sweetness creates a harmony in the grappa. The bitterness originates from acids in the grapes, substances in the wood of the barrel, from copper residue from the *alambicco* or from poor caramel colouring (if it is quickly coloured in this way).

Sour
Grappa contains organic acids which are enhanced during ageing when the alcohol is transformed. The acids are difficult to detect but play a vital role for both the structure and completeness. Without acid a grappa is flat.

Salt
Grappa has no salt when it comes from the *alambicco*. Salt should not be present at all. The water used to dilute the grappa is the source of the salt, if any.

DEFECTS

Grappa that is produced in non-industrial conditions is a product of artisans and as such, can in rare cases contain defects. This is due to the vinaccia being stored incorrectly and/or the incomplete separation of the *testa* and *coda*. Defects in the finished product are a sign of sloppiness or lack of skill as most faults should be detected and corrected in the distillery.

Unwanted odours

Mould
This is the worst thing that can happen to a grappa, as it cannot be fixed by the distiller. The defect is due to over-long or careless storage of vinaccia.

Vinegar
Vinaccia is constantly threatened by bacteria that produce acetic acid, acetate aldehyde, ethyl acetate and other substances that can give grappa a sour taste.

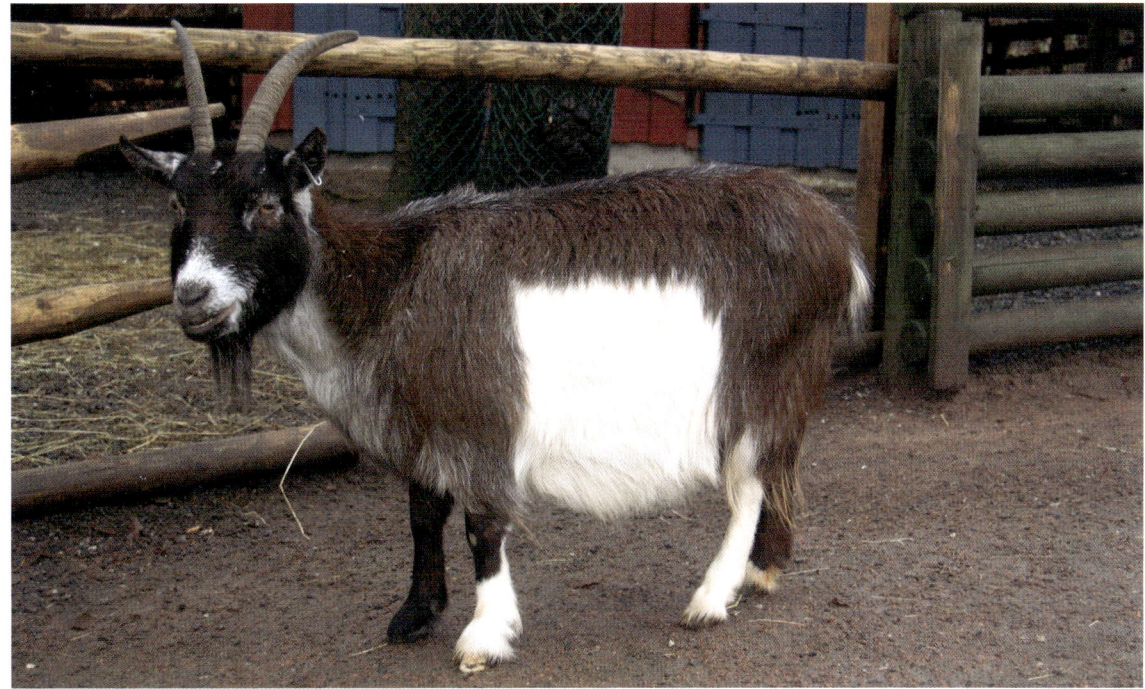

Rotten Egg
This is caused by sulphides from vinaccia that has not adequately fermented. The sulphur usually disappears as it reacts with the copper of the *alambicco*.

Goaty
A nauseating and rotten odour resulting from butyric acid and ethylbutyrate. It is created when sugar in the vinaccia ferments without oxygen.

Sour-cabbage
This rotten smell occur when proteins in vinaccia are attacked by bacteria.

Wax, resin, sweat...
These less pleasant odours from ethyl esters expose defects in the storage of the vinaccia as well as non-skilful distilling.

Rancid
This is often caused by unsaturated aldehydes (even in very low concentrations) which are created as the vinaccia is preserved.

Pungent odour
A *strong* accent, almost physically painful sensation caused by ethanol and other very fleeting, pungent substances.

A true *pungent* odour is a typical sign of poor distilling and incorrect storage of the vinaccia

Undesirable flavours

Woody
Caused when a grappa is barrelled for too long, or where the wood is too young or the type of wood is unsuitable.

Metallic
A taste that is transferred from the *alambicco* or metal vats.

Bitter
This is caused by, amongst others, butyric acid and proprionic acid formed as a result of poor storage of the vinaccia.

Acidic
This occurs when the *coda* is not correctly removed.

A MODEL FOR GRAPPA TASTING

There are various models for how grappa can be tasted and various criteria to judge it by. Below are a few examples of terms and criteria from a model developed by Luigi Odello – enologist, author and leading figure in Italy and the Centro Studi e Formazione Assaggiatore (an organisation for food and wine tasters).

APPEARANCE

The judgement of the clarity of a *grappa giovane* or the colour nuances of a *grappa invecchiata*:

Clarity – *Limpidezza*

Examples of descriptive words:
Crystal clear, mountain spring, hay-yellow, amber, mahogany...

AROMA

All aromas must be pleasant. Just one bad odour can disrupt the balance of a grappa. Firstly, a grappa's aroma is judged via the nose – *nasal* – and then subsequent aromas from the mouth and throat – *retro-nasal*.

The aroma is divided into the criteria: *Intensity, Finesse, Expression* and *Fragrance*. Try to describe these with your own words, otherwise each judgement become "just words".

Intensity – *Intensità*

The judgement of an aroma's total quantity and strength without taking into account its quality or alcoholic content.

It is a measure of how "great" the grappa or the bouquet is.

Examples of descriptive words: Powerful, rich, strong, striking, insignificant, bland, weak, undetectable, dead.

Finesse – *Finezza*

The nose's judgement of the aroma's quality and also a description of the associations it creates.

Examples of descriptive words:
Quality: Exquisite, excellent composition, good, average, low, bad, appalling...
Associations: Distillery, grapes, vinaccia, vineyard, cellar, dried fruit, spices, tobacco, forest, petroleum, rubber...

Expression – *Franchezza**

The judgement of each individual aroma's contour and distinctness, and their interplay; their "expressiveness" and the "distance" between them. A subtle aroma can emerge against the background of alcohol and work perfectly together. An extremely distant but still unpleasant aroma can disrupt any pleasing aromas.

Examples of descriptive words:
Clear, distinct, harmonious, true, pure, untainted, diffuse, unclear, discordant, disturbing...

*e.g. frankness, honesty, sincerity...

Fragrance – *Fragranza*

This is an important – and debated – criteria that describes a grappa's complexity and the richness of the bouquet. The judgement of the fragrance refer to aromas reminiscent of fruit, flowers and other natural scents.

Examples of descriptive words:
Wonderful, rich, intense, rose, raspberry, apricot, grass, raisin, fruity, spicy, fresh, chocolate, coffee, stable, leather ...

FLAVOUR

The judgement of aromas once the grappa has been warmed in the mouth and they reach the nose a second time *retro-nasally*. By comparing the *retro-nasal* experience to the initial *nasal* experience you get a complete picture of a grappa's true personality, that is – does the first impression hold up?

Harmony – *Armonia*

Flavour is mainly decided by the balance between aroma and alcohol strength. A harmonious and rounded grappa fills the mouth without violence, creating a pleasant warmth and leaving a cloud of aroma after each mouthful. A pungent grappa that burns cannot be harmonious.

Examples of descriptive words:
Perfect, well-balanced, harmonious, considered, round, unbalanced, edgy, spiky, aggressive, sharp, pungent...

Persistence – *Persistenza*

The judgement of the pleasant aroma persistence or length after swallowing. A good grappa should last one minute at the least.

Examples of descriptive words:
Long, even, short...

PIANOFORTE® – AN ALTERNATIVE MODEL

This is a suggestion for a simpler model with fixed descriptive expressions inspired by the international Italian musical language. These tonal instructions are usually used to describe the *feeling* and the *tempo* with which the music should be played.* Why should not aromas and flavours be expressed in a similar way? Tastes and flavours create strong emotional sensations – and flavours have movements. You may precede your judgements with a *meno* (less), *poco* (little) or *molto* (much) to more finely tune your opinion.

APPEARANCE

For *grappa giovane*

• Clarity – *Limpidezza*
Is the grappa crystal clear?

Brilliante　**Meno brillante**
(brilliant)　*(less brilliant)*

For *grappa invecchiata*

• Colour nuances – *Tonalità*
What is the colour of the grappa?

Leggero　**Moderato**　**Pesante**
(light)　*(moderate)*　*(heavy)*

AROMA

• The aroma's intensity – *Intensità*
(regardless of quality)

Tranquillo　**Allegro**　**Agitato**
(calm)　*(fast)*　*(agitated)*

• The aromas' quality – *Finezza*

Staccato　**Legato**　**Delicatissimo**
(separated)　*(joined)*　*(very delicate)*
not so delicate　*delicate*

Describe your associations to the aroma in your own words.

TEXTURE

• Alcohol strength – *Forza*
How does the grappa feel in the mouth?

Forte　**Fortissimo**　**Con fuoco**
(strong)　*(very strong)*　*(fiery (negative))*

FLAVOUR

Does the flavour increase after swallowing? Is there balance between the aromas and the alcohol?
Does the grappa taste better or worse than it smells?

• Harmony – *Armonia*

Diminuendo　**Spianato**　**Crescendo**
(decreasing)　*(even)*　*(increasing)*

• Aroma – *Profumi*

Describe the grappa's flavour in general?

For *grappa giovane* (freshness)

Adagio　**Andante**　**Vivace**
(slow)　*(walking pace)*　*(lively)*

For *grappa invecchiata* (depth, saturation)

Semplice　**Espressivo**　**Appassionato**
(simple)　*(expressive)*　*(passionate)*

Describe your associations.

AFTER TASTE

• Finale – *Finale*

Subito　**Smorzando**　**Sostenuto**
(sudden)　*(fading)*　*(sustained)*

---

* The descriptive Italian expressions are in the masculine form as used in musical score. Otherwise, words used in conjunction with (*la*) grappa have the feminine forms.

Nocturne op 15 no 1. Frédéric Chopin. Edition Peters.

A splash of distillation history

The art of distilling is ancient. Truly ancient if you believe the legends that already in Mesopotamia (present day Iraq) around 3,500 B.C. the knowledge existed to distil perfume and possibly alcohol. Some say, the Chinese knew the secret of distilling around 200 B.C. However, neither of these are proven. To get really close to the truth of the origins of distilling, we need (as is often the case) to go back to the Greeks. The Greeks brought the knowledge of distilling to Rome before it was lost with the fall of the Roman Empire . However, under the Byzantine Empire – that succeeded the Roman Empire in the middle of 1,000 A.D. – the Arabs preserved the knowledge and also refined the technique of distilling.

The principles behind distillation were proclaimed by Aristotle in 300 B.C. as the solution to the problem of extracting fresh water from salt water. He suspended a lambskin just over the surface of the ocean. When the skin was damp the water that was wrung out was fresh! This evaporation technique was used by Alexander, a student of Aristotle's, during his maritime conquests.

The first recorded description of a distilling process was in 100 A.D. by Dioscoride, a Turkish botanist. "Distilling is imitating the sun that evaporates the water from the earth and returns it as rain."

Distillation of alcohol
Some sources indicate that alcohol was produced in southern Europe during the Middle Ages but it was not until around 1,000 A.D. that development really took off. Previously, distilleries were used to capture an essence or soul of a substance. They were searching for a mystical dimension. Minerals, substances from fauna and flora and even human blood were used to create rosewater, perfume, pigments and many other products for medical use. The oldest Italian references to alcohol production are medicinal, from the renowned medical school of Salerno in Sicily, around 1,000 A.D. Although it is entirely possible that they could extract the alcohol from wine, it is not known if they were the first to attempt this.

The first in-depth description of manufacturing techniques were from the thirteenth century by the Italian doctor Taddeo degli Alderotti, the French doctor Arnaut de Villeneuve and the Spanish doctor Raymondo Lullo. The *Bibliothèque Nationale* in Paris also has handwritten descriptions from the fourteenth century of a distilling apparatus *bagnomaria* (using hot water) and a *bagno di sabbia* (using sand, that was heated). The most common models had pumpkin-shaped boilers – *cucurbita*. The best was called *ambix* – a Greek word which became *alambicco* in Italian and in other countries was given a similar name.

The fifth element
Alderotti, Villeneuve and Lullo are seen as the founders of *brandy* – which is a distilled wine – however, they viewed the drink as medicinal, a wonder drug called *acqua della vita* – a water that prolonged life. Villeneuve called it *eau de vie* and Lullo called it *aqua ardente* – burning water. "A heavenly and divine drink which, with the sun's help, emerges from the grapes" wrote Lullo, believing that he had found Aristotle's fifth element – *quintessence*. The origin of quintessence and life was the sun. It was the heat of the sun that gave life and cured disease. Alcohol spread the heat of the sun in the body, therefore alcohol was medicinal.

From the church of Tempio Canoviano in Possagno, Veneto.

"A heavenly and divine product of the grapevine, that every day soaks up the heaven's moisture and with the sun's help, lets it emerge from the grapes."

Raymondo Lullo, Spain, 13th Century

The first printed book on the subject

Doctor Michele Savonarola (1384-1462) from Padua claimed that it was technically impossible to create quintessence or *acqua della* vita from wine. However, he did not doubt the existence of such a drink. In his treatise *Libellus de aqua ardente*, published in 1484 after his death, he states that by distilling wine a few times *aqua ardente* is created "with the colour and consistency of water with the effect of fire." He continues to say that an *acqua della vita* however, demands up to ten distillations, which is in principle technically impossible. *Aqua ardente* "that is used in medicine" therefore belongs to the fourth element – fire – and only resembles *quintessence*.

Ponte Romano, the very old bridge in Voltaggio, in the Gavi wine district of Piemonte.

Savonarola was aware of the risks of alcohol and warned of possible misuse. In *Libellus de aqua ardenti*, which is considered to be the first printed book on spirits, he scientifically analyses the manufacturing techniques used, a distillate's contents, the effect on people and its assumed healing properties.

A little misunderstanding?

Savonarola writes that the term *acqua della vita* or *acua vitae* refers to *vite* and not *vita* (life). *Vite*, which means grapevine, was also a name for the distillation apparatus: the characteristic spiral-shaped pipe resembled quite simply the twists of a grapevine! In any case, alcohol was increasingly used as *the water of life* in the context of enjoyment. Already by the 1500's there were many distilleries in Italy and Venice became an export centre from where "burnt wine" was distributed throughout Europe.

Grappa's long journey

The essential difference between grappa and brandy is the raw material. Brandy is created from wine – a liquid – and grappa uses the grape skins – a solid. Compared with wine, vinaccia is poor in alcohol, containing only a third of the alcohol in wine, at most.

Vinaccia used to be the only product a grape grower could keep. The wine must went to the local lord or land owner as a tax. Ordinary people did not drink wine; but by diluting the vinaccia with water they got a wine slop called *vinello*, which at least resembled wine. In Tuscany, Veneto and Piemonte they also used to boil the grape skins, as early as in the thirteenth century. The result was a strong drink that gave the body warmth, released them from the daily drudge and eased the senses in the winter darkness. A sort of primitive grappa, poorly regarded. Dante and Petrarca considered it vile, as did the noblesse who drank wine.

It was back in these times grappa started its long journey to respectability.

"O alcohol, thanks to you I have been able to live twenty years longer."

Doctor Antonio della Scarparia, at the age of 80, extolling the powers of acqua della vita. Italy 15th Century.

The term *alcohol* comes from the Arabic word *al kuhl* – a fine black powder used as eye make-up. In the 1500's, a doctor by the name of Parcelo began to use the term alcohol to refer to any fine powder. Eventually, the term came to mean the finest part of a liquid. Distilled wine was called *alcoholi vini* or *spiritus vini* – the wine's finest part or its "spirit". The word for the distillation apparatus *alambicco* (in Italian) and similar expressions in other languages comes from the Greek word *ambix* denoting the distillation bowl.

Interiors from the museum of Antica Distilleria Laura Mazzetti in Altavilla, Piemonte.

A cheap food-stuff

The earliest documents regarding the distillation of vinaccia are from the 1600's. The authors were Jesuit monks like Francesco Terzi Lana from Brescia in Italy, the Spanish monk Miguel Augusti and the German monk Atanasio Kricher. These writings allowed the art of distilling vinaccia to spread to the wine growing regions of Europe where the tradition of distilling using grape skins, or diluted grape skins, as a raw material still lives on today. In Germany for example, it is called *Tresterbrand*, in France *marc* and in Spain *orujo*.

The methods and techniques were refined, in no small part thanks to the observations of Michele Savonarola. In the 1700's, the first Italian equipment specifically for grappa distilling was developed. Inspired by industrialisation and steam power, the development of the still continued throughout the 1800's. However, how grappa was consumed did not change – it was still seen as a cheap and high-energy food-stuff for the lower classes.

Grappa becomes typically Italian

That grappa came to be a typical Italian phenomenon is partly due to the arrival of the distillation column. It was developed by the Florentine Baglioni in 1813. This apparatus allowed continuous and efficient production of alcohol with excellent purity. The problem was that the raw material had to be fluid, in other words – vinaccia would not work. But the technique was perfect for brandy. However, by diluting the vinaccia to get *vinello* it was possible to distil it using this new method – which also eliminated the risk of burning or other damage to the grappa*.

But the new technology did not really take off in Italy – where they continued to distil using vinaccia. Perhaps it was due to lack of resources or simply because they wanted to keep producing grappa in the traditional way. In the 1800's the Italians also defined their grappa and gave it a national identity. At the turn of the 20th century, there were around 100,000 grappa distilleries in Italy.

The great leap forward

The First World War was a breakthrough for grappa in Italy. From its simple roots as a basic consumable for the poor masses, it spread through the soldiers around the country. Grappa was introduced to new consumer groups and was suddenly used for pleasure. The improved distilling methods and industrial techniques smoothed the rough edges that changed a raw peasant drink into a common acceptable beverage.

However, it was not until the 70's that the grappa industry started to market itself and position grappa as an interesting, dry and flavoursome alternative to sweet liqueurs and the established digestifs like Cognac and whisky. In 1973 *Distilleria Nonino* launched the concept of *grappa monovitigno* – grappa from a single grape variety – which further boosted both the business and the market. Product development escalated and it was not exclusive to the grappa; new, increasingly elegant, interesting bottles and labels began to emerge. This, together with a popular rise in interest in the environment and tradition, further increased grappa sales. This was not just in Italy – international interest in Italian food and wine had already begun to open doors.

The journey to respectability from a simple blood-warming drink and cheap inebriant to a cultural beverage with gastronomic flair was complete.

*Marc – the French "grappa" – is primarily made this way by distilling diluted vinaccia (i.e. without the skins).

A view from Grappa – the mountain (1,776 m).

The term grappa

Bassano del Grappa in Veneto is a town with a genuine grappa tradition. It was here that the oldest, still operating distillery in Italy *Distilleria Nardini* was founded, which to this day remains owned and operated by the same family. However, the town's name has little to do with the drink *(la)grappa*, rather the mountain *(il monte)* Grappa which is in the vicinity. It begs the question: did the mountain get its name from the distillate or the distillate from the mountain?

Regardless, when it comes to the term *grappa* there are many explanations as to its origin. Most believe that there is a connection to grapes and grape classes, which in Latin are *rapus* and *grappulus* respectively. Similar terms can be found in the local dialect, *raspo*, *graspo* and *graspa*. *Raspo* is the modern Italian word for grape stalk; whilst *graspo* is a dialectical variant from Veneto and Lombardy that means grape or grape class (the proper word for grape class is *grappolo*). *Graspa* can mean both *grappa* and *vinaccia*, depending on where it is said.

There are also a plethora of old local words for grappa, such as *sgnapa* (Veneto), *grapa* (Lombardy), *cadevia* (Trentino), *branda* (Piemonte) and so on: *sgrappa*, *trapa*, *sgagne*, *raspa*, *brasca*, *ega de vita* (northern Italy) as well as *brusca*, *fumetto*, *aqua de veta*, *spirito abbardeenti*, *filu* and *ferru* (central to southern Italy).

Piazza Libertà, Bassano del Grappa. The church of Saint John the Baptist (Chiesa di San Giovanni Battista) was built in the 14th century and reconstructed in the 18th. It used to be referred to as "buszia" ("lie" in local dialect) because of the striking contrast between its imposing exterior and the small interior.

Other distillates

Armagnac
  A French brandy from the Armagnac region. It is aged in oak barrels.

Brandy
  A term used for all distillates made from wine – *eau-de-vie* or "the water of life". The name, brandy, comes from the Dutch word for burnt wine *brande wijn*. Aged in oak barrels.

Calvados
  A French distillate made from apple cider from the region Calvados in Normandy. It is aged in oak barrels.

Cognac
  A French brandy from the seven famous areas of Cognac in Bordeaux, among them Grande and Petite Champagne. Aged in select oak barrels.

Rum
  A distillate made from sugar cane. Industrial rum is made from molasses. The name rum possibly comes from *saccarum* (Latin for sugar cane) or from pirate sayings for commotion (rumballion) or revolution (rumbastion). Rum can be bottled directly or aged.

Whisky
  A distillate of grains such as corn, barley and rye depending on the type of whisky. Aged in oak barrels. The name originates from the Gaelic word *uisquebeatha* (water of life) which became *uisque*.

Vodka
  A distillate made from wheat, rye, corn and even potatoes. Originally an unflavoured distillate today it is often flavoured. The name vodka, comes from the Russian word for water, *voda*.

Acquavite d'uva
A fruit-distillate made by yeasting the whole grape. It is often confused with grappa (which is an *acquavite di vinaccia*). *Acquavite d'uva* is less alcoholic than grappa, more fruity and elegant in taste, and more expensive.

Foreign "Grappa"
Distillates made outside of Italy with vinaccia or diluted vinaccia (i.e. *vinello*, without the grape skins) as the raw material:

Austria – *Trebern* or *Trebener*, Bulgaria – *(Rakia) Dzhibrova*, France – *Marc*, Former Yugoslavia – *(Rakia) komovica*, Crete – *Tsikoudia*, Croatia – *Lozovaca*, Cyprus – *Zivania*, Germany – *Trester (brand)*, Hungary – *Törköly (pálinka)*, Luxembourg – *Wainheffen*, Macedonia – *Tsipouro*, Spain – *Orujo*, Switzerland – *Trasch*

Il viaggio

THE JOURNEY

My trip to Italy was planned down to the last detail – except for where I would go, who I would visit and where I would stay. I knew next to nothing about grappa, besides perhaps that coffee and grappa worked well together as an elegant way to finish a good dinner – a *digestivo*, as the Italians say. But before I had reached Italy's borders I had doubled my knowledge. Grappa can also rescue a bad dinner.

As I sat in my car on that clear October morning, the air was crisp and new, like the first day of school with its vibe of uncertainty and hesitation. But there was also something comical and nerdy. I was about to start a voyage of discovery, but I was not sure what I was looking for. My mind was set on a soul. The soul of grappa. How was this supposed to end? Would it even begin at all?

After just a few hours I already felt like I was in Italy as I drifted through a part of Denmark that reminded me of Tuscany. The clear blue sky suspended above the rolling hills with its spider's web of haze. The hilly horizon was broken here and there by seemingly hastily initiated and interrupted cypress avenue projects. The golden light deepened gradually and when the sun disappeared – somewhere south of Hamburg – the fields around me turned dark red. Tuscany was still with me in northern Germany. Very strange.

Grappa had baffled me for many years. I was a sporadic grappa drinker, enjoying a glass from time to time, usually out at restaurants but mostly when travelling abroad. I did not understand the taste but there was something there that appealed to me. The confidence, obstinacy and more than a hint of cheek. Grappa does not try to ingratiate itself or charm. It is as if it is hiding a secret. Like a cat smiling in the sun

Grappa does not come to you. You must come to the grappa.

How should grappa taste? What is a "good" grappa? Questions coursed through my head on the road south. What does "taste good" mean? A juicy, red apple is good; raspberries are good as are ice cream, sun warm tomatoes, freshly baked bread and steaming pasta. Most people agree that these taste good, if they are not hindered by dietary restrictions or principles. Now what about a mouldy cheese? Does its aroma make you want to sink your teeth into it? Does an oyster immediately make your mouth water? Admirers say that

Vigo di Ton, Trentino.

these taste "good" but this is only a lazy way to express their intense experience. What they mean is that a flavour exceeds the norm or the most commonly experienced "goodness". A delicacy does not necessarily taste good.

> *Dov'è la stazione della metropolitana più vicina? – Where is the nearest underground station?*

The beginner course in Italian kept repeating itself through the car's speakers, at a droning pace. Occasionally it broke my thoughts and caught my attention. I listened, catching a phrase, playing it back, thinking it over, and making it my own: *Dov'è la distilleria della grappa più vicina*

If you expect something to taste bad, it probably will. Likewise, if you think it will taste good, it probably will not be bad. Our thoughts, images and associations affect how we experience what we consume more than we think. Have we perhaps already made up our minds before we open our mouths? Our senses of taste and smell are fragile and susceptible to suggestion. One careless word, an off mood at the table can be all it takes to numb our senses in a second.

> *At the restaurant: Ho appetito. Vorrei polpette di carne e patate bollite – I am famished. I would like to order the meatballs and boiled potatoes.*

Hey? Come on! Here I am on my way to Italy, to *la cucina italiana!* My newly purchased language course is not quite up to date – the last thing I would be ordering is Swedish-style meatballs and boiled potatoes in Italy!

> *Posso pagare con traveller's check? – Would it be possible to pay using traveller's cheques?*

Grappa is like blue cheese and oysters. That is why you should not expect a grappa to taste "good". You have to decide to acquire a taste for the odd flavour of a grappa. And what differentiates a good grappa from a bad one? What is the true soul or essence of grappa, or does it exist?

The following evening I ended up in a hotel in a little Bavarian town. Soon I found myself wandering along looking for hanging ironwork beer hall signs. I passed by an Italian café but I was hungry so I kept going and ended up in a *stube* (beerhouse) with a cold German beer and pork fillet which was not very tasty. On the way back to the hotel my stomach was upset and I thought of the little Italian café I had passed on the way. An espresso and a grappa put me right again. A *digestivo* saved the dinner and Grappaland was only a day away.

TRENTINO–ALTO ADIGE

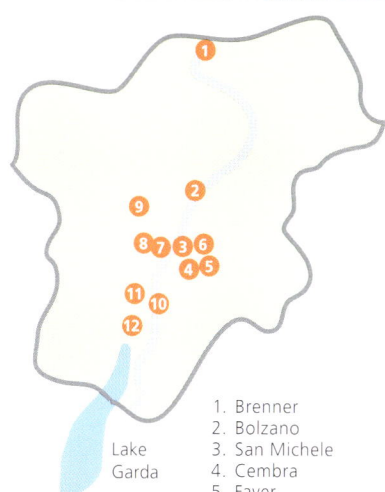

1. Brenner
2. Bolzano
3. San Michele
4. Cembra
5. Faver
6. Faedo
7. Mezzocorona
8. Mezzolombardo
9. Ton
10. Trento
11. Lago di Massenza
12. Riva del Garda

The road through the Alps and the Brenner Pass into Italy was dizzyingly beautiful. In Alto Adige, the Italian Tyrol I began to regret not choosing the road less travelled with its winding valley roads past villages and churches far below the motorway. I exited a little north of Bolzano, which landed me in the centre of town before I found a road that ran parallel to the motorway and by pure chance found the *Strada del vino* heading south. I drove through the idyllic villages of Ora, Cortina, Magre and Salomo but none made me stop. From the heights of the

Distilleria Dalpas in Vigo di Ton.   *Ivo Dalpas.*

DIST. BERTAGNOLLI
GRAPPA DI MOSCATO
– GIOVANE –

motorway I could see everything I desired but close-up it seemed to have vanished. Perhaps I was just indolent and feeling lack-lustre as one can sometimes be when searching a room for the night. In any case, I was in Trentino, close to the one and only point on my itinerary: the Cembra Valley.

I drove to Mezzocorona, checked in at a hotel, went to the Bar Centrale around the corner and ordered a coffee and grappa. "*Si, la grappa è nostrana*" replied the woman behind the counter, Yes, it's a locally made grappa. *Nostrano* is a key concept within *la cucina italiana* which emphasizes the local aspect of cooking. She also gave a few names of local distilleries.

Distilleria Bertagnolli, a renowned producer and exporter, lay in the middle of the wine growing regions around Mezzocorona. Maybe here I could get my first lesson in grappa and hopefully in English. But it was Saturday and the distillery was closed. In any case I now knew where it was. Even though a distillery has a smoking chimney and many of the locals convince you that you can not miss it, this is not always the case. I would learn this lesson time and time again.

The next distillery on my list was *Dalpas* in Ton, so I headed off through the town of Mezzolombardo and up the mountain. A road sign with Vigo di Ton sent me off to the right on a road that climbed alarmingly up the mountain side. A woman stood in front of a house so I stopped and backed up a few metres before asking: "*Mi scusi, signora. C'è una distilleria della grappa in vicina?*"

Distilleria Bertagnolli

Bertagnolli was founded in 1870. It is the first distillery in Europe to use a fully automatic bagnomaria system, i.e. an artisan technique in large scale. The temperatures inside the alambicco are controlled by a computer, to guarantee a perfect and homogenous grappa. The distillery has six discontinuous copper alambicchi, each with a capacity of 3,200 pounds. The equipment is made by the legendary master copper maker, Tullio Zadra, who improved the distilling techniques and accomplished the bagnomaria method in the 1950's and 60's. The typical method for Trentino grappa.

Forward, she said, and straight on to Toss di Ton and ask for *Signore* Fedrizzo Stefano. So on I drove into the sky. A kilometre felt like five on those snaking roads past peculiar houses – but the view was enchanting. What does close mean? Eventually I arrived at Toss di Ton and drove until the road ended and then continued on foot. I found a distillery, but not the one I was looking for. *Distilleria Fedrizzi* was brand new but I found nobody there. I exchanged a few words with the sympathetic Saint Bernard behind the bars. "I know what you've got in your keg" I said.

Distilleria Dalpas

I turned back and found distilleria Dalpas, which lay right after the sign for Vigo di Ton. *Vendita Grappa* it said on the door – grappa for sale! My journey's first real distillery visit! I hesitated for a few seconds while I flipped through a few Italian phrases in my head. The distiller himself, Ivo Dalpas, opened the door and showed me into the little shop which

DISTILLERIA DALPAS
GRAPPA DI TOLDEGO
– GIOVANE –

also housed the bottling machine. Ivo does everything himself. From what I could understand he makes two sorts of white grappa: *grappa giovane* 43% and 47%, and some g*rappe aromatizzate*. I tried the less alcoholic of the white grappa. Difficult, I thought, sharp, aggressive, burning and basically awful. But the sun shone on that bright day and I was a novice. I bought a bottle anyhow and wondered how it would taste once I was back in Sweden, whether the journey would change the flavour.

The distilling equipment, the *alambicco*, was housed in a type of garage. A cloud of flies hovered like static over the large open tub. Was *this* the raw product, the vinaccia? The strange aroma and the earthy scene was surprising, to say the least, to this city-boy.

I HEADED DOWN INTO THE VALLEY AGAIN and over the River Adige on the hunt for a new room and a more strategic base for my future day trips. I wound my way through the roads of San Michele without success and, as I was not in the mood for another mountain adventure, I decided to drive towards the Cembra Valley. As I headed south the soft afternoon light enveloped me. Where was I going, really? Will I find somewhere to stay? Will I find anything to write about? The road ahead began climbing again against my will but suddenly, there it was, the Cembra Valley spread out before me in all its beauty. Quickly my doubts vanished.

I passed through a few villages on the edge of the valley and hoped that Cembra was as a central as I first thought. The first hotel signpost caught my eye and I decided to stay at the *Europa* for two nights, at least. The concierge was very helpful, telling me about the local distilleries. He even drew a map with points of interest for me. I took a short walk with the camera and on the way back through the village I met a man busily closing a large, heavy, wooden door. Before he had closed it completely I caught a glimpse of a steel tank. No harm in asking *"Buona sera. Quest è una distilleria della grappa?"* (Good evening, is this a grappa distillery?). No, answered the man in blue overalls, *faccio il vino* (I make wine). Then he launched into fast – *veloce* – Italian before I managed to say: *"Mi scusi, parlo solo un po' d'italiano"* (I'm sorry, I only speak a little Italian). He slowed down for a few seconds before it was veloce again.

He was a charming man and to talk slowly in your own language is an art. During my travels I noticed that there are very few people who can manage this on demand. Italians are not alone in this habit.

The next day I decided to visit the *Pilzer* distillery in Faver, a small village situated a bit further in the Cembra Valley.

I Piramidi di Segonzano. The Pyramids of Segonzano. As the rain drops hit the ground, the water causes an erosive action that slowly has dug out the strange formations in the slopes of the soft mountain. The top stones were once on the ground and have acted as "starters" of each pyramid. A more imaginative explanation is that the Pyramids already existed in the ground – the rain has merely uncovered them!

Distilleria Pilzer

I peeped through the huge panoramic windows of Distilleria Pilzer – the inside looked like an art gallery. Vincenzo Pilzer, the father, met me with a branch in his hands and introduced me to his son, Ivano, who lives on top of the distillery with his wife and children. The older son, Bruno, works at the distillery as well but is also a lecturer at the *Istituto Agrario di San Michele all'Adige*. The two brothers are enologists, in other words wine specialists, both educated at the institute in San Michele. Later I received my first practical and very scientific lesson in grappa at the institute's distillery by *maestro* Bruno Pilzer himself.

DISTILLERIA PILZER
GRAPPA DI SCHIAVA
– GIOVANE –

I spent one night with Bruno and Ivano at the distillery. Production was in full swing with vinaccia from Lagrein grapes that looked like mashed beetroot. The place smelled of cooking berry jam. And while the production continued we discussed grappa. Bruno prefers to taste the grappa in balloon-like wine glasses that captures the aromas. He thought that *Schiava* grapes make the best grappa "it tastes like grappa should" he said. "Something quite different from the grappa slops that the supermarket sell. I think Grappa is best suited to contemplation, after dinner or, why not, after skiing."

We tasted the *Gelbe Moscato*, also a white grappa. Ivano thought it was too aromatic. I thought it was awesome. The taste remained in the mouth for at least 15 minutes, but of course there is a boundary between too many floral flavours and too little grappa. Then we tasted a Traminer, with delicate flavour – slightly abrasive.

DISTILLERIA PILZER
GRAPPA COLLECTION
– GIOVANE –

"The type of grape used in a grappa *invecchiata* – aged grappa – doesn't matter as much," he said. "Often it is made up of a mix of grapes and the taste of the grapes is camouflaged by the wood of the barrel. Colour also affects the tasting experience and brown can infer a cognac association. Don't think of cognac when tasting grappa. It is a very different type of distillate. Grappa should be like the water from the mountain tops – crystal clear."

The law in Trentino requires the reuse of the distilled vinaccia. "We boil it in the yard and let the buyers come and get it. We don't get much for it," said Ivano. "But anyway, the seeds become cooking oil and pellets, the rest becomes compost or maybe bird and pig food."

Ivano Pilzer.

Bruno and Vincenzo Pilzer.

Ivano and Bruno Pilzer.

Like an art gallery. Distilleria Pilzer in Faver, Cembra valley.

The Alpine Bar that includes the Distilleria Giacomozzi Renzo.

One Giacomozzi brother attending.

AT THE HOTEL I THREW MYSELF DOWN at the computer with my bundle of notes and a digital camera full of photos. As a way of relaxing while I worked I put on Chopin. By sheer chance, the date was October 17th, the date of his death. Or was it a coincidence? The waltz in C sharp minor sang to me: da DI – DA da-grappa-di – da-grappa-dey…

Distilleria Giacomozzi Renzo

Distilleria Giacomozzi Renzo is on the other side of the valley in Segonzano. *Piramidi di Segonzano* is a peculiar natural phenomenon of ancient towers and pinnacles sculpted by natural erosion from the clay of the mountain. It is reminiscent of Gaudi's nightmarish cathedral in Barcelona.

The distillery and the restaurant *Alpine Bar* are high up in the village. The door to the restaurant was open, inside was dark and cool and there I found the twin brothers Pietro and Paulo Giacomozzi at the bar. A man entered and ordered a grappa. He nodded at me with a happy grin. I tried the same and bought a bottle – a lightly toned *grappa invecchiata* (aged grappa). The distillery was not in action this day but I was invited to catch a glimpse of it another day. And I heard something that sounded like "the grappa institute". A grappa institute! Here! My trip had really started off fine.

DIST. GIACOMOZZI
ANTICA GRAPPA DELLA VALLE DI CEMBRA
– INVECCHIATA –

The distillery of Istituto di San Michele.

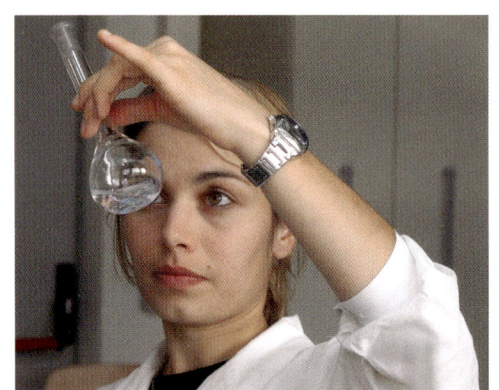
Lorena Sigismondi, the laboratory.

Istituto Agrario di San Michele all'Adige has a vineyard that produces wine, its own grappa distillery and a laboratory for chemically analysing grappa to define, amongst other things, a grappa's origin. This testing ensures that a grappa that calls itself Grappa Trentino or Grappa Alto Adige fulfils the relevant specifications.

Distilleria Paolazzi

The distilleria Paolazzi Vittorio is right on the edge of the Cembra valley in the village of Faver. I found Vittorio Paolazzi covered in smoke, winching a basket heaving with steaming vinaccia. He distils using the vapour method a vapore diretto. He showed me the alambicco and was very enthusiastic when I brought out the camera. Only a small part of the production is sold under Vittorio's own label; most is delivered to distilleries and bottlers who do not distil but acquire finished grappa to make grappa blends.

Distilleria Pojer e Sandri

Azienda Pojer e Sandri is a model complex for production of wine and grappa. It is situated in the village of Faedo, high between the Cembra Valley and the Adige river. The western Dolomites (*Le Dolomiti occidentali*) provide a majestic backdrop.

Mario Pojer sang the praises of the Dolomites' white chalky earth and Cembra's brown porphyry and pointed above Faedo. "There, the mountain has broken up and exposed a layer of earth that is the best possible soil." That is where the best grapes grow, guarded by balloons painted with bird-of-prey eyes – an Australian trick. The summers are warm here but the Dolomites give off heat which creates a kind of convection current that drags the cool air off Lake Garda. This the grapes also like.

DIST. POJER E SANDRI
GRAPPA TRAMINER
– GIOVANE –

"Because we make the wine ourselves, we have full control of the distillation and the quality of the grappa. Like a formula one race," said Mario. "Our vinaccia is fresh direct from the winery, with no vinegar, residue or bacteria. All the aromas are still there and before we ferment the green grape skins we take away all the stalks as well as the seeds. We started using this technique in 2003 and we were the only ones doing so in Italy at the time. This year we are doing the same with the red grape solids, but after the fermentation of course."

"The seeds contain wood and oil that can transfer a bitterness to the grappa, especially if the seeds have been in contact with the skins for a long period of time; storing periods of two to three months are not uncommon in the industry. During this time the yeasting process starts and the raw vinaccia deteriorates. That is why industrial grappa producers must "clean" their product many times over in tall rectification columns. We don't need to do that. Now we use only three plates in our distillation column – before we had ten."

DIST. POJER E SANDRI
GRAPPA PINOT NERO
– GIOVANE –

"Our oxygen-free pressing technique in the winery also gives a better vinaccia," said Mario. "The process is completely contained and the oxygen is replaced with nitrogen to reduce oxidation of the grape skins. The result is both a clearer wine must and greener grape skins, which results in a better raw product for grappa. And the wine's aroma is improved. Usually white wines get bitter after seven to eight months, whilst ours are still fresh and crisp. This method is also healthier as the antioxidant in the skins, which otherwise disappear, are transferred to the wine. The technique is patented and wine universities from all over the world come here to study it. The interest is due to the possibility of

The bottles with a bright content contain must for white wine produced in an oxygen free process. The must in the other bottles are made traditionally and show the effect of oxidisation.

Mario Pojer, Distilleria Pojer e Sandri in Faedo.

reducing the use of sulphur in the process. At the University of Bordeaux they are thinking of replacing the sulphur with glutathione, which is one of nature's most powerful and most common antioxidants. Just 10 milligrams of glutathione per litre will preserve a wine for three to four years. Our technique preserves a good quantity of the glutathione present in the grape, sometimes to a high degree. In our Sauvignon for example the level is around 60 milligrams per litre."

Distillation is managed by computers. "One person can control everything," said Mario. The system is programmed with 30 years of experience and uses precision curves and profiles for differing grape varieties. The *testa* and *coda* are separated automatically: a photocell reads the alcohol meter and activates the valve. The finished grappa has 75 percent alcohol which is then reduced to 48 percent with the addition of pure water from a granite mountain spring . No extra sugar, no additives, flavours or aromatic substances. "Grappa should be grappa – made with fresh grape skins and pure water!"

And how about *grappa invecchiata* I prompt. "No, No," said Mario Pojer. "Grappa should be white, a concentrate of the aromas of the vinaccia only. That is why it shouldn't be aged in oak barrels. Grappa is not like Calvados or some old cognac."

Around two in the afternoon I left *Distilleria Pojer e Sandri* and set south towards Trento and the "Grappa Institute" someone had told me about. I was looking for a complete list of grappa distilleries. And a "Grappa Institute" can not be that hard to find in Italy, can it? When I asked at the attendant at the Trentino exit tollbooth about the "Grappa Institute", his shoulders answered with a shrug. The brown signs pointing towards the tourist information office took me on a swirly ride to the town centre. It was getting late, a little after four, but suddenly and almost magically a small, but straight, street opened up in front of me that led directly to the heart of the city. Like the Mediterranean parting. I found a tight parking space, tailored for my car size, right on the main street and only 100 metres from my destination. In a flurry, I grabbed my bag and camera, ran through the entrance, and checked my position with two gentlemen on my way up a before reaching the door. I rang the bell. Not a sound from inside. Well, at least I thought I knew where the "Grappa Institute" was situated. Later I found out that there are many "Grappa Institutes" in Italy, one in every grappa region of importance: *Istituto Nazionale Grappa*.

I took a breath in the car while checking my computer for directions southwards. A sharp rapping startled me. It was a police officer in full uniform who delivered a barrage of abuse at me. I did not understand a word but I got the gist. I was not supposed to park here! I tried to placate him in broken English (at such times it is unwise to have any knowledge of Italian). Clear off he motioned. It seems I had inadvertently parked in the middle of a *centro storico*, which means historical centre and implies a constant traffic jam. In all Italian cities there are beautiful old streets built for horse and carriage that require special licenses and permission for cars. In future, I would take care to avoid all *centri storiche*. Go, go, go, the police officer motioned after me.

Where would I go now? Mario had recommended a hotel beside a small lake called Lago Lagola, not far from Lago di Toblino at Santa Massenza. At Lake Toblino are five small and old family-owned distilleries that he had advised me to visit. All bear the name of Poli but have no connection to the famous *Poli Distillerie* in Veneto. In the 1990's Jacopo Poli from Poli Distillerie started claiming the sole rights to the name. "Our distillery is the oldest Poli on the market, we have invested millions in our trademark – no others should profit from it. We don't want consumers running the risk of getting the wrong grappa."

"But Poli is our name too" they responded at lake Tobino – "and we have also been making grappa for generations". Four of them have ceased writing "Poli" on their labels. One still do.

I left Trento heading east toward Lago di Toblino but soon broke off the search for distilleries. It was getting late and I fixed my mind on Lago Lagola and the hotel. The road was still very dramatic and I cheered myself up with the prospect of the arrival. A cold beer. A warm bed. I took a left and headed into the mountains that were getting darker and darker. I found the lake wreathed by autumn leaves. Everything was still – really still. I knocked on the door of the very closed hotel. From the empty lobby I heard a voice saying that there was a hotel 12 kilometres up the road. Like an automaton I continued to drive until I slammed on the brakes and turned back. Towards Lake Garda! Then down the mountain into the veils of fog in second gear using the clutch pedal for breaking and acceleration. I finally made it back again to the road, one that probably had been laid out by the Romans. The mountains looked the same in their time.

It was dark when I finally arrived at a sign saying: *Riva del Garda* 2 km to the right, and Torbole to the left. "Beach" (*Riva* in Italian) sounded pleasant and soon I was driving in-between hotel balconies and sailing yacht masts. Here at least the hotels were open. I began modestly and looked for signs *Camere* (Rooms). An older lady showed me a room and began to haggle with herself. I explained there was nothing wrong with the price; it was the room

Lago di Garda. Lake Garda.

I did not like. Then I thought, in fact I am at the famous Lake Garda and my accommodation needed some style. I continued to look for a hotel a little further away from the lakeside and found only two. One with a room with almost a whole window and the second with nice facilities. *Avete qualcosa più economica?* Do you have anything cheaper? I decided to try Torbole, and I had not even made to third gear before I was surrounded by bright hotel neon lights. I was tired and hungry and headed directly after check-in to a restaurant across the street, ordered a beer, pizza and a carafe of red wine. I went through the day's notes and practiced Italian verb conjugations, pondered and savoured. I thought the *grissini* tasted of grappa! As did the beer and the accompaniments. I came to think of the aroma of Pilzer's still and Mario Pojer's words about the impact of climate, rock and soil. Now I was tasting Trentino! I wondered how Veneto would taste and Tuscany and Piemonte.

In "centro storico" of the city Malcesine on Lago di Garda.

To my right was a German couple and to my left sat two English ladies and a little further off were a group from France. The English ladies belonged to a bus tour group. We talked about English TV-series, ABBA and grappa. When I ordered an espresso and a *grappa nostrana* they asked if I was a wine expert.

As it was, I needed a few days to write down the recording and notes, get my pictures in order and pull all the facts together. Riva del Garda seemed good but I wanted to find another hotel further to the eastern shore with more serenity and inspiration.

The next morning the road wound its way past the shores of the lake that I could only imagine in rain and fog. There is something special about sitting in a newly packed car after breakfast, feeling well rested and fed and wondering – where to now?

VENETO AND FRIULI

I PASSED THROUGH VILLAGE AFTER VILLAGE and passed many hotels and many signs declaring rooms for rent. Most were probably closed for the season. As usual one misses opportunity after opportunity. Sometimes one just does not feel like stopping. After all it is a homy place one is looking for. It has to feel right – it has to look nice. I arrived in Malcesine and was hooked by the foggy silhouette of the fortress tower.

I began my search for a room at a "family-hotel". The price was

VENETO
1. Malcesine
2. Verona
3. Vicenza
4. Montegalda
5. Padova
6. Rosà
7. Bassano del Grappa
8. Asolo
9. Valdobbiadene
10. Conegliano
11. Vas
12. Treviso
13. Venice

FRIULI – VENEZIA GIULIA
1. Pordenone
2. Castions di Zoppola
3. Udine
4. Percoto
5. Cividale del Friuli
6. Nimis
7. Trieste

reasonable but the room was permeated with smoke. That sent me on the road again and I looped out of town and made a second entrance and parked in front of the imposing ski-lift. Nearby, I found a small, fresh and cosy hotel, *Ariston*. My sunny room had fresh flowers, chocolates on the dresser and a balcony facing the mountain, with villas and cypress trees. *La prendo* (I'll take it) I said. I then explored the decorative, narrow streets near the *centro storico* – by foot. I bought bread, cheese, salami, beer, wine, some chips and sweets at a little shop where tourists do not go, outside the medieval idyll.

    I stayed three nights in Malcesine and caught up on my notes. The interview with Mario Pojer in German was only an hour and fifteen minutes long but took me all day to write up. I also planned the rest of the trip. First to the east towards Veneto past Vicenza and Verona, then to Bassano del Grappa and the region Friuli in Italy's far east. Next I would turn west again towards Lombardy and

Malcesine with its towering "Il castello Scaligero".

Piemonte, before heading south along the Mediterranean through Liguria to Tuscany and finally to Trentino via Bologna to visit some friends. I also hoped I could take in the Poli distilleries at Lago di Toblino and the Bertagnolli distillery in Mezzocorona that I had missed.

In the evening, a couple of friends called to tell me about the Bob Dylan concert they had been to in Gothenburg. He had played Desolation Row – a song I had never heard live. In all, they thought the concert was good. I doubted it. I exchanged a few text messages with my wife on the cell phone before I returned to my work on the computer. I put on un unheard album by a Swedish singer but after listening I was indifferent. Lots of rock'n'roll, lots of will-power but something was missing – melody. There must always be some kind of melody somewhere…When I had turned off the light, it struck me that the music was actually causing resistance. It was not flattering or charming. Like grappa – there is something there for you, but you have to get it yourself.

On a Sunday morning I said goodbye to my hosts at the hotel – mother and daughter – and carried my ridiculous load of luggage and bags to the car and drove off under a leaden sky. The towns I passed looked dull in the rain and I could hardly see the lake either, and suddenly I was washed out on the *autostrada*. The weather was not enticing so of Vicenza and Verona I only saw the highway exits.

The road from the highway to Bassano del Grappa looked as if it ran straight through the outskirts of an industrial city. On the map all towns look like idyllic little villages and the roads seem to run through fields of green. The reality is something else. But as I approached the town the sun almost peaked through the fog and the landscape came alive with colour. I thought, "I am in Italy after all" and the reassuring feeling returned once again – I had chosen the right destination. I parked near the *Ponte vecchio* (the old bridge) and then walked *through* it and past the distilleria Nardini's boutique at the abutment on the *centro storico* side of the city, in search of a place to stay.

I pounded the streets up and down without even seeing a hotel sign.

The bridge Ponte degli Alpini is said to be the world's oldest wooden bridge, even though it has been repeatedly rebuilt after damages from wars and the current waters of the river Brenta. The latest reincarnation occurred due to the actions of Gli Alpini – the legendary Italian commandos – whose efforts on the Grappa mountain were decisive for the outcome of the First World War, La Guerra Grande. The bridge used to be called Ponte Vecchio (The old bridge). Its origin dates back to 1571.

I continued "eastwards" before I finally passed the city walls and exited the old town. It felt good to be among the avenue of trees with autumn painted leaves and the traffic whizzing by. On the other side of the street I spied a hotel displaying four stars on the wall. I approached the green uniformed reception staff. He was finishing off a phone conversation in English and I asked for a room and a price in the same language. He showed me one but I was not convinced of the value. Instead I went to a hotel close by called the *Brennero*, with three stars. *Il padrone* (the owner) Zaccaria Profeta did not speak any English but convinced me easily of a room including *collazione* (breakfast). The fourth star, announcing "We speak English", obviously has a price. Thus, studying a little Italian before the trip is a good investment. Zaccaria said he could guarantee two nights. *Posso vedere la camera?* May I take a look at the room? *Certo!* The room was little but quiet and facing a courtyard.

"In March of 1834 George Sand, who loved the waters, the valleys and the mountains of Italy, as well as its works of art, stayed in this coffee house and spent a delicious morning in Bassano, a memory she regarded as one of the greatest fortunes that could happen to a traveller… (From the book "Lettres d'un voyageur").

Distilleria Nardini, the oldest grappa producer still in action. Note the sign announcing that George Sand – the once very celebrated female writer who lived together with Frédéric Chopin – was once here.

I collected the car and drove to the entrance of the hotel and there Zaccaria stood with a trolley, took my luggage and gave me a free ticket for parking just a hundred metres down the road. When I returned there was a freshly printed list on the reception desk. "I got 26 hits on local distilleries on the web", Zaccaria said.

Later that evening, on the way back to the hotel after a dinner at a restaurant he recommended – I noticed on the wall right next to the hotel a big sign DITTO NARDINI – the name of Italy's oldest, still functioning distillery. I stepped into the *bottiglieria* the bar and bottle shop, on the ground floor and addressed one of the staff. "Yes, the distillery was once located in this building but nowadays it is located outside of town." Their first distillery was founded in 1779 by Bartolo Nardini and was located by the old bridge. Mario Pojer had told me that Bartolo was born in the village of Faver in the Cembra Valley.

Strange coincidences.

Distilleria Capovilla is situated in the village Rosà right outside of Bassano del Grappa. "Just follow the signs to Padua", the parking attendant informed me the next morning. I found Rosà without a problem – road signs in Italy are fairly close together, but a sign to a distillery? I did not see one. *"Mi scusi, dov'è la distilleria Capovilla?"* I asked an older man. He looked confused. Strange. This distillery is world renowned, at least in the grappa world. I showed him the address and he began pointing and giving instructions until he finally opened the car door and stepped in while I quickly moved the computer away from the passenger seat. "Drive in the opposite direction," he said, "Turn here, straight, *non così veloce*, not so fast. *Si fermi qui!* Stop here. *A sinistra, per favore.* Left, please." He told me that he had been a police officer. A narrow, tree-lined road led to a farm out on a field. He looked contemplative and then signed to me that he wanted to get out. "Let's continue a little further," he suddenly said. But he did not get out until he was sure I had found my way.

Nonino – the inventor

Distilleria Nonino in Percoto, Friuli, has played a significant role in the development of grappa from an Italian concern to a distillate of world standing.
In 1973 Nonino created the grappa *monovitigno*® or *di vitigno* – i.e. grappa from a single grape variety that has been stored separately. This had not been done consistently anywhere before. The *grappa monovitigno* became instrumental in raising the quality of grappa and blazed a trail for the future. The first grape to receive the attentions of Nonino was a local white grape called Picolit, which was quickly followed by other local varieties such as Ribolla Gialla and red grape varieties such as Schioppettino and Pignolo. Some of these varieties were in danger of extinction and to salvage these Nonino created the award "Risit d'Azur" ("golden vine" in the Friul language) and in 1978 obtained EEC authorization to re-start the cultivation of these grapes.

In 1984, Nonino launched their next invention, *l'acquavite d'uva*, which is a distillate made from fermented whole grapes, not just the skins which is the case with grappa (which is a *acquavite di vinaccia*). Previously in Italy distilling whole grapes was forbidden. Any fruit could be distilled but grapes were to be saved for wine production. Nonino managed to convince the Italian Minestries of Industry, Agriculture and Health to pass, a new law allowing distillation of whole grapes; thus made *acquavite d'uva* came true. This distillate is reminiscent of grappa, at least from the outside, and is often confused with grappa. However *acquavite d'uva* usually has a lower alcoholic content than grappa and is more fruity and elegant in taste. It is also more expensive than grappa; the fresh grapes cost at least ten times more than the vinaccia, and only yield double the volume.

Distilleria Capovilla in Rosà.

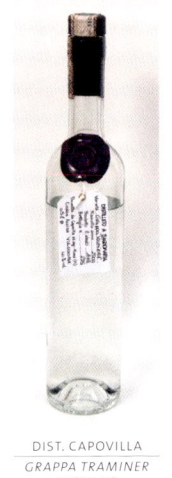

DIST. CAPOVILLA
*GRAPPA TRAMINER
– GIOVANE –*

Distilleria Capovilla

Vittorio Capovilla reminded me of Sean Connery; a senior James Bond. He is dynamic, charismatic, driven and passionate. He started his distillery in 1986 after a career as a racing car driver and as a salesman for wine technologies in German and Austria. In his free-time he used to devise his own mechanical solutions.

"I was educated as an engineer," he said, "but grappa distilling is a craft I taught myself. There wasn't even a tradition of grappa distilling in the family." At that moment he was processing vinaccia from Traminer grapes – an aromatic green grape. The skins smelled soft and fresh. I wanted to bury my hands in them.

Gianni, as he is called by his friends, showed me his *alambicco* which he had in no small part built by himself. "Those two boilers," he pointed, "are over 70 years old and made in Germany, based on the Italian tradition but modified in a *bagnomaria* technique. "I suddenly realised the difference between the methods of *bagnomaria* using a double-boiler, and *vapore diretto* using vapour. In Trentino I had so far only seen *bagnomaria* stills, except at Paolazzi in Faver. Here in Veneto, steam is the tradition.

Capovilla has developed his own method which is a combination of *bagnomaria* and *vapore*. The boiler has a double wall for processing

The maestro from Monte Grappa – Vittorio Capovilla.

steam (*bagnomaria*) which indirectly warms the vinaccia that are placed in four baskets (*vapore*). The steam is also pumped into the boiler through the base so that the distilling point can be reached more quickly. However, the hot steam does not come in direct contact with the vinaccia. "That's why we add approximately 15 litres of water in the boiler," Capovilla said. "The base acts as a barrier. The steam warms the water which then starts to boil creating a gentle steam. Then the generated steam is cut and the process continues from the heat of the double boiler wall, which allows the steam inside the boiler to flow gently through the grape skins."

"Lower temperatures, gentle pressure and slow processing are vital," said Capovilla. "A maximum temperature of 100 degrees Celsius in the boiler and the steam should not exceed 102-103 degrees. That way you get more aroma from the vinaccia. Industrially produced grappa is done at higher pressures with steam that is around 110-115 degrees. It is more efficient that way. My process takes around seven to eight times longer, which means that my grappa costs about seven to eight time more to produce."

DIST. CAPOVILLA
*GRAPPA MOSCATO GIALLO
– GIOVANE –*

Each boiler can take around 500 kg of vinaccia and the process takes around four hours. One load of vinaccia with an alcohol content of around five percent produces around 25 litres of pure grappa which is diluted with as much water to create a grappa of consumable strength. "I have built a blender which is, in principle, a refrigerator," he said pointing to his Casco-patent. "When the grappa is chilled undesirable elements are released that the blender then absorbs."

Capovilla identifies the *cuore* by feel – using his sense of taste and smell. "You can't just use alcohol strength as the only indicator," he said. "Methyl alcohol has no aroma or flavour, it is present all the time even if most of it disappears in the *testa*. When I can't sense anything disturbing I know that *cuore* is coming. Therefore, good grappa is a matter of taste. I would never add sugar or any other flavouring, although they are permitted within certain limits. For example a *grappa monovitigno* – grappa from a particular grape – can be "improved" without a mention on the label!"

DIST. CAPOVILLA
*GRAPPA DI AMARONE
– GIOVANE –*

After the grappa is distilled it rests for a few years in steel vats for the balance and harmony of the grappa. But he does not use oak vats as oak is a type of flavouring. Finally, he will number the bottles and signs them just like lithographers – the artist Capovilla.

He beats his own path and often against the mainstream. He burns

Right in the middle of the two giants Poli and Nardini – the Poli grappa museum and Nardinis shop at the old bridge of Bassano del Grappa.

Asolo. An idyllic medieval town with an ancient history; the Romans called it Acelum. Many famous artists have worked and got inspired here, Ernest Hemingway and Igor Stravinsky to name but two.

for the artisan-style of grappa making and was not shy in his criticism of the larger industrial distilleries. "For me grappa is a *digestivo*. The problem is that almost all the industrial grappa is produced under high pressure and high temperatures. The oil in the seeds is then released into the grappa. This activates the stomach acids, so how can they call it a digestive?" he philosophised.

After my meeting with the maestro from Monte Grappa I drove to Bassano del Grappa and back in time about one hundred years. First I visited the Nardini's boutique at *Ponte degli Alpini* (Ponte Vecchio's name today), where the distillery originally was founded in 1779. They informed that in two days I would be welcome to attend a tour of the distillery. After this I headed across the street to the beautiful Poli grappa museum. There I was, literally in the centre of the grappa world – right in the middle of Bassano del Grappa, caught in the energy field of two famous grappa brands. I was also right in the middle of the tourist hordes. I could really sense the emission of the power these distilleries possess. It is not strange then that it is grappa labels like these you often see around the world.

The following two days were a mixture of sightseeing and taking photos. During breakfast *padrone* Zaccaria gave me a handbook about *Esagono sei città* (six cities) and a few tips. I started off by taking a drive up the Monte del Grappa. The view was spectacular but the fog thickened and made me turn. On the way down I encountered a paraglider who hovered just beside my side window for a few seconds. Once I had reached the foot of the mountain I continued on to Possagono with its elaborate temple creation called *Canoviano*. The sun was obscured behind clouds and the light made the marble look as soft as velvet; enticing you to strech out and caress it. The day ended at Asolo, an idyllic medieval town with seductive alleyways and exclusive villas occupying majestic Tuscan vistas.

The church of Tempio Canoviano in Possagno was based on ideas of the local artist Antonio Canova. The building expresses three different periods of the Italian history: Greek civilization (the Dorian columns reminiscent of the Parthenon in Athens) Roman culture (the main building reminiscent of the Parthenon in Rome) and Christianity (the apses reminiscent of old Christian basilicas).

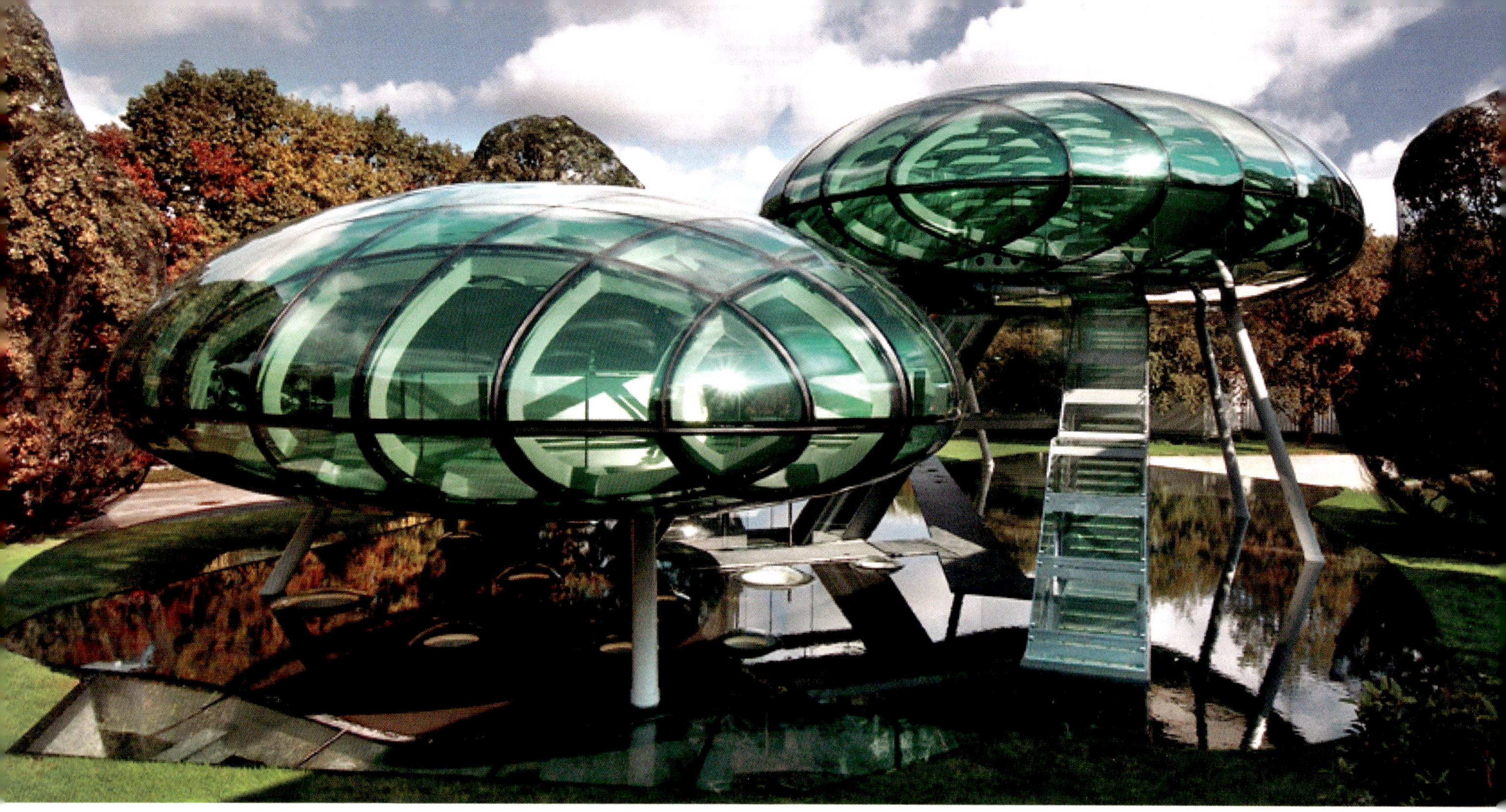

Le bolle – Distilleria Nardini's ethereal conference room and laboratory.

Distilleria Nardini

DISTILLERIA NARDINI
GRAPPA AQUAVITE
– RISERVA –

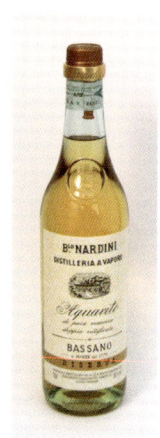

I found the Distilleria Nardini without any problem but due to the fog I missed the round-about despite the previous day's practice run. I had met Giovanna Caprioglio only two days prior at the Nardini's *grapperia* downtown and now she was there to meet me. We began with the two impossibly futuristic glass bubbles that seem to hover weightlessly in veil of mist, *Le bolle.*

"They symbolise the drops of grappa emerging from the *alambicco*," she explained as we were transformed into a green dreamscape. "The first bubble is our laboratory and the other is where we hold our corporate meetings." The complex is adjacent to the currently inactive grappa plant. Production would not begin until the end of November and would continue through March. For this reason the spectacular auditorium was created, where a captivating and very professional

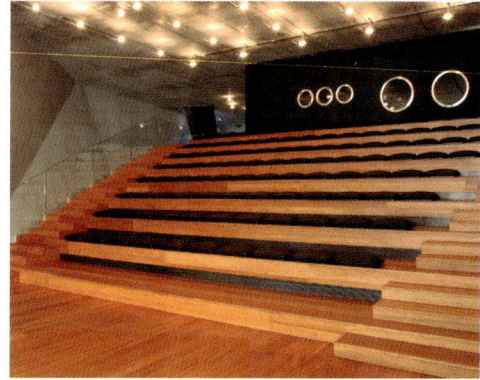

The auditorium.

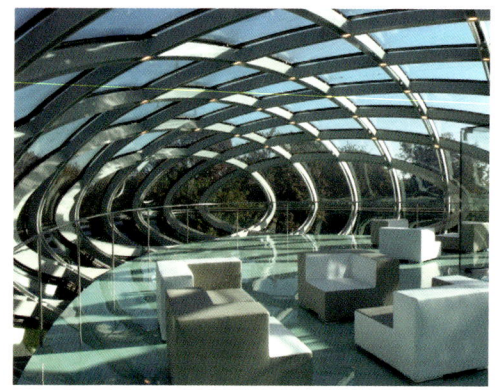

The conference room.

Le bolle – the bubbles – were designed by Italian architect Massimiliano Fuksas. The building was opened in 2004 in conjunction with Nardini's 225th anniversary.

presentation was shown, with a strong emphasis on the benefits of rectification and filtration. After the show we went to the tasting room where all Nardini products are on display.

"At the moment we are collecting the vinaccia," said Giovanna as she showed me the forty, cement storage units of seven cubic metres each. "Each silo, of which we at present use only 20, contains around 200 tonnes of vinaccia. Our Monastier facility in Treviso is six times larger; however it all ends up here for bottling. In total, we process around 40,000 tonnes of vinaccia every year and produce approximately 4 million litres of alcohol. Over 95 percent of our production is devoted to grappa; the rest is made up of digestives and liqueurs. White *grappa giovane* or *grappa bianca* is our best seller, with oak-aged grappa only making up around 12 percent of our sales."

"Nardini Grappa Bianca is produced from vinaccia from red and white DOC grapes selected from the foothills area of the Veneto and Friuli regions", she explained. "However, the skins are combined in varying proportions and even the grappas from the two facilities are blended. In the end, the blend and the quality are consistent due to continuous monitoring from the laboratory."

DISTILLERIA NARDINI
GRAPPA AQUAVITE
– GIOVANE –

I BIT INTO A JUICY APPLE as I drove towards the *Distilleria Brunello* in Montegalda. I looked out for road signs and estimated distances in order to follow the verbal directions I had received from Zaccaria. Even though the directions did not quite match reality, I managed to find my way to Montegalda – and only 800 metres from my ultimate destination. Unfortunately, I did not realise this. The language barrier would trick me once again. I thought the lady in *l'edicola* (the newsstand) said "80 metres to the left". So when I did not find it, I turned back but found a man in the stand who told me "eight kilometres to the left". The first seven kilometres I drove more or less blindly, of course, and then through one village and then another. But no distillery. It was already half past two in the afternoon and I was starving, but I pressed on. I eventually did a hasty u-turn somewhere and decided to stop at a house. The owner nodded and told me it was five kilometres *that* way – back to Montegalda! It was the "*cento metri*" that had confused me. It means "100 metres", but I thought it sounded more like kilometres. *Ottocento metri* – 800 metres. It would not be the last time I would mix up these concepts. Stress, coupled with an unfamiliar dialect can sometimes create an irritating misunderstanding; entertaining in hindsight though.

The back yard of Distilleria Brunello in Montgalda.   *Maestro Giovanni Brunello.*

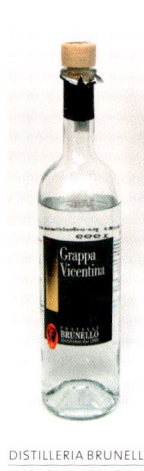

DISTILLERIA BRUNELLO
GRAPPA VICENTINA
– GIOVANE –

Distilleria Brunello

As luck would have it Distilleria Brunello was in clear sight from a little road café, so I managed to fit in a cup of coffee and two cheese sandwiches. I drove the car to the rear of the building and stepped into the distillery. A young man, whom Zaccaria had told me about earlier in the morning, was working in the distillery shop and greeted me in English. He soon returned with *maestro* Giovanni Brunello. Together Giovanni and his brothers Paulo and Stefano Brunello make up the fifth generation to have run the distillery since 1840.

Brunello is an artisan-style boutique still on a slightly larger scale with two boilers *a vapore* in the Venetian tradition. The boilers can each hold 500 kg of vinaccia and run independently of each other.

"Most of our vinaccia comes from grapes grown in this region," Giovanni said. "Like Cabernet Sauvignon, Merlot, Barbera, green Muscat and Tokay. Almost two thirds of our grappa is produced from red grapes. We also produce grappa made from the grape skins of the Tuscan wine Brunello di Montalcino. One fifth of our grappa is destined for export."

"The art of making grappa is partly about knowing what a good vinaccia is but also about knowing your *alambicco*," Giovanni explained. "It is also about using low temperatures, around 105°C, and low pressure, about half an atmosphere. I define the *cuore* on the basis of alcohol strength." The equipment is sealed and the authorities forbid any type of tapping of the grappa – even for tasting purposes.

ON THE ROAD BACK TO BASSANO DEL GRAPPA I pondered the distilleries' equipment and storage spaces tangled in the lead seal web of the Guardia di Finanza – the Italian tax and police authority. All stills are different but have two things in common. The lead seal and the Contalitri – the ever-present typically shaped volume meter that tirelessly counts the drops for the state.

Giovanni Brunello discharging baskets of used vinaccia. A distinctive feature of the distilling method a vapore diretto.

And the possibilities for each *maestro* to "taste-test" the distillate obviously varies from place to place.

For breakfast the next day Zaccaria welcomed me as usual with a hearty, *"Buongiorno il professore!"* The time had come to say goodbye to him and his wife Lucia and continue eastwards to Conegliano. "I have tried to get in contact with the professor at the "Grappa Academy" in Conegliano." said Zaccaria as he handed me a piece of paper. "I can also check out a few hotels for you if you like." I thanked him but told him that I would find myself a room when I got there.

As I wanted to reach Conegliano as soon as possible, I took the highway to Padua. The traffic around Venice began to get heavy and *la nebbia* (the fog) was as thick as the trucks around me. But sooner or later the sun found an opening in the clouds, and her impact on the landscape and my mood was just as striking every time. My first impression of Conegliano was as when you have arrived in a strange town on a Saturday afternoon, hungry and have no place to stay. I ended up at fairly dull hotel in a room with a wall-to-wall brown carpet. I wanted to say no but I was too tired.

I rang the "professor at the Grappa Academy" without success. I got into the car and decided to let intuition lead me in the right direction. A winding road up the hillside took my fancy and I was finally breathing fresh air. Up on the mountain I drove through villages and wineries ablaze with a riot of colours in the afternoon sun. I saw cyclists and other tourists on the little white road but not a single pension or place to stay. I had decided to spend some time in this area. Another road took me down again and right into the *centro storico* and suddenly

"Il padrone "Zaccaria Profeta of hotel Brennero. Note the sign on the house corner to the right.

MONTE GRAPPA TU SEI LA MIA PATRIA is cut in stone on the base of the soldier's statue. "Monte Grappa you are my homeland". Hard, heroic and decisive battles were fought in the city of Bassano during the First Word War. Afterwards, in recognition the city's name was changed to Bassano del Grappa from Bassano Veneto. Note the Nardini name on the wall.

the car was right outside the tourist information centre. I went in and began speaking with the personnel in my fumbled Italian. What an idiot! In a tourist information centre! I instantly changed to English in the middle of a sentence and the clerk immediately gave me a brochure with hotels and B&B's in the area: "What do you think of this one? Should I call and ask for you?" he said. It was just as before, when the sun was breaking through. Soon he had a response from a vineyard. "I need three nights' accommodation to start with" I said. It was in the middle of the wine district in a village called Valdobbiadene. Two policemen stepped in and warned me that a car parked just down the road was about to get a fine. They had spied mine on the pavement just outside. That is excellent service too!

Valdobbiadene. Another name that would take me three days to learn how to pronounce, spell and remember.

In the evening I lurked about the centre of Conegliano looking for a place to eat. My lunch of yoghurt and fruit in the car had worn off a long time ago. I thought about heading into a pizzeria, when I saw a sign *pranzo* across the street, meaning lunch. The bar was called *Rio de Janeiro* and was very South American style: bright, naked lights, strong colours and sparse. A regal-looking and beautiful woman, Brazilian I presumed, ran the bar with charm and tough control. "*Si accomodi!*" take a seat, she said before listing the dishes of the evening. I chose the *lasagna*. "*E una birra alla spina*" – a beer on tap. Then I looked around surveying the scene like a novelist looking for ideas. In one corner some older men sat drinking wine, or was it grappa? A woman met up with a couple of young men in football uniforms, they disappeared and then returned. They were served wine from the tap. Two miserable types made an entry with a crash. One was on crutches and the other was carrying a cupboard box. They spoke harshly and the man with the box started to argue and bluster. He started rummaging in the box before pulling out what seemed like a fresh mushroom. The waitress arrived with my meal. As I wandered home in

The symbol of Valdobbiadene "Il Campanile" – the Bell Tower with its sun-dial on Piazza Marconi. First erected in 1767, seriously damaged during the First World War and then restored.

the warm autumn evening I came across the two figures in an alleyway and heard the grunting of the mushroom man behind me.

My sharp nose led me back to the hotel without a problem. I rely on my steady inner compass, like I used to when I was at sea many years ago and strolled the streets of cities like Casablanca, Tripoli, Alexandria and Bombay, as it was called then. Before I left Conegliano the next day I located a laundromat or *lavanderia a gettoni*. I started by looking over the machine and the bilingual instructions. A little, old lady started an animated description of it operation. "Wait, I will just get my laundry first," I said and I returned with my plastic bags in seconds. She chose a machine and the program and even helped me load the machine. While we waited for the clothes to tumble dry I asked for directions to Valdobbiadene and held up my road map. She walked out the door and returned with a man from the street who could give me an explanation. First I should drive to Pieve di Soligo and then straight ahead, *sempre dritto*.

I found it without a hitch; the landscape became more and more beautiful with each passing kilometre and the vineyards more frequent. I thought: how strange. All the coincidences that seem to guide me. Why was I driving on this particular road, in this direction, at this very moment? Something overwhelmed me, which I did not quite understand. I was out searching for a deeper understanding of grappa – or just out on a trivial grappa safari or whatever – but yet something, or someone, was trying to push me in the right direction. Or maybe it was just the colours of the landscape and the afternoon sun that filled me with happiness.

Welcome to Valdobbiadene – *città del vino* – which also is the name of a larger area surrounding the city. I realised this as I came across the sign again and again before I actually reached the town. I rang the owner who met me in her car and piloted me to her B&B called *Aries*. There were no other guests in sight so I had the entire house to myself. Paola Agostinelli showed me around the kitchen where a wood stove crackled and two bottles of *spumante* stood waiting on the table. "*Il fuoco a legno è allegro*", said Paola, a retired teacher. "*Allegro* usually means merry," she continued and I believe she meant that "fire from wood is cosy." She showed me my room on the second floor, a small room with a tiny desk and a bathroom outside the door. She then showed me a room with a double bed, a writing desk and a toilet inside. "*Preferisco questa camera. La prendo.*" I prefer this room. I'll take it.

Paola was born in the mountains, in a little village called Rocca Pietore on Marmolada Montagna high up in the Dolomites. Her husband Luciano was born on the vineyard. Previously, there was also an *osteria* from where the family sold their own wine by the bottle or by the glass. In the eighties, as there was an increasing demand for Italian wine, they stopped the dairy and put all their energy into grape growing. Today, Luciano grows Prosecco grapes almost exclusively, which are then sold to a wine cooperative that makes *Prosecco* – the region's famous *spumante*, sparkling wine. Only *Prosecco* from Valdobbiadene or Conegliano can use the DOC stamp.

The Prosecco grape with its ancient origins dating back to Roman times, is harvested by hand over an eight to ten day period in September. Friends and relatives of Luciano and Paola give a helping hand; only handpicked grapes will do for the Prosecco DOC. During winter, the vines are pruned and the earth is turned and fertilised. In April, the vines begin to sprout and little by little the small and precious, very sweet, golden grapes emerge. The wine grown for the household includes Fragola, also called Americana or Concord grapes. There are also Clinto grapes; however they are no longer allowed for wine making due to their very high tannin content.

Paola spoke to me in measured Italian sprinkled with an English word or two when I needed it. Luciano opened a bottle of the vineyard's *spumante* and we toasted. Paola gave me the name of a good and price-worthy restaurant in the area – with the exotic name The Darling – and when I came home in the evening the dogs started to bark. My hosts peaked out through the window, Luciano with a bottle of grappa in each hand. We sat in the kitchen, talking and tasting the grappa. "*Fa el resentin con la grappa!*" as they say in Veneto. Rinse your coffee cup with grappa!

The crowing of a rooster woke me up next morning. The sun was blazing, the wood fire crackled merrily in the kitchen and breakfast lay waiting on the table. Afterwards, I went out and photographed the yawning cats. I worked, wrote up clean copy of my interviews, sent some text messages and visited the fridge in the kitchen. I stretched out on the bed and gave in to that sleepiness that no one can withstand. After about half an hour I woke and started working again on the computer. That evening while enjoying a little bread, cheese, salami and a beer, there was a knock on the door. It was Luciano with an offer

My room.

"Aries Agriturismo" in Valdobbiadene. One of the many B&B facilities you will find all over Italy, where you live, eat and drink local food and wines, and at a good price.

of Fragola wine. The wine had a lovely aroma and tasted divine; like the kitchen, like the whole place. Luciano told me that they used to dilute the wine with water. "That's not gonna happen in Sweden" I said.

As usual, the stove crackled *allegro molto* when I stepped into the kitchen the following day. An older German couple sat by the table. They had arrived on Saturday night in a car and a motorcycle. That day I continued to work and read Italian until late in the evening. The kitchen table offered more space to work – and for my legs under it – than the tiny table in my room. Every now and again Paola would look in with a small knock and a soft *permesso?* "May I come in?"– and then asked if I might like a cup of coffee.

I took a mid-afternoon walk and followed the road up the slope aways. Here the grapevines stay in straight, neat rows regardless of the incline of the hills. In the distance I could hear a hunter's gun firing at rabbits or pheasants. Paola had also told me that around here there were plenty of edible mushrooms. Bonfires of leaf litter here and there created wisps of smoke that mingled with evening over the landscape. Dogs started barking when I neared the farmhouses. On the road back I stopped by a spumante factory. Sleek like Braun HiFi equipment from the seventies. I returned to the kitchen table, the work and the music. A mixture of Beethoven's piano sonatas and Mozart's piano concertos. I felt very at ease and comfortable in myself, by myself – it felt good. My hosts looked in on me and Paola told me about two *maestri della grappa* she knows. "It has been 30 years since I spoke to either of them," she said but she would try to get in touch with them and set up a meeting. It was no inconvenience for me; I had already decided to stay longer. Valdobbiadene would become the central point for my visits to Veneto and Fruili.

Despite the fact that it was a Monday between the weekend and the All Saints Day holiday (*Tutti i Santi* or *Ognissanti*), Paola managed to get hold of Luciano Brotto. On Wednesday we were invited to visit *Scuola Enologica di Conegliano* and meet this *maestro* who is both responsible for distillery

The walk to St Eustachio Abbey in Nervesa della Battaglia.

education and for running the distillery *Centopercento* in Giavera del Montello. There is also a *Distilleria Brotto* in Cornmuda owned by Luciano's brother. I devoted the rest of the Monday to following the brown *Guerra Grande* signposts, a kind of *strada del vino* or *route de vin*. The autumn atmosphere complimented sad memorials with eerie names such as Morario della Battaglia, Nervesa della Battaglia and Isola dei Morti – the Isle of the Dead.

Once back at the pension I washed the dust from the road away with a pilsner and enjoyed a *prosciutto cotto* (cooked ham) with tomatoes from the garden, not sun warmed but lovely anyway. Maps and brochures kept me company when I heard a *permesso* from Paola at the door. She wondered if I wanted to go to church with them. I declined the offer. Today I regret it. I must have been weary. How often does the chance come up to go to an All Saints Day Mass in a little church in Veneto?

St Eustachio Abbey in Nervesa was founded in the 11th century. Located in a strategic point of observation on the river of Piave, it was reduced to ashes in 1918 by German and Italian artillery. The abbey used to be an extraordinary example of Roman-Benedictine architecture.

Isola dei Morti – The Island of the Dead – today also called Isola Verde – The Green Island – because of the park's rich vegetation. Famous brands are often old. The tyre of this canon wheel in Isola dei Morti was made by Pirelli.

All Saints Day. The German family were moving on, home most likely. Now the kids were also there and they sat squeezed into the car with their mother. The father sat armoured in leather on his shiny Harley Davidson that seemed to twitch like a stallion beneath him. I had never seen a happier man.

Since it was a holiday, I wanted to visit some of the magnificent Venetian palaces. I also wanted to drive along the *Via Postumia*. A certain kind of spirituality comes over me when I drive or walk on ancient pathways and roads. It soon became apparent to me that yesterday's excursion should have been made today – the roads were empty.

Villa Sandi-Cassis. The splendid pomp started early at the gates and, at this time of the year, the luscious splendour and the secrets lurking behind the bars seemed to exisit for me only. There was not a living soul in sight. The closest neighbour was a big wine trader with a similar name. The gate was wide open

Villa Sandhi-Cassis from 1622. *Villa Rinaldi-Barbini from 1663.*

so I snuck in, only to be curtly turned away by two agitated ladies. It was the first incident during the trip, not counting the unreasonable constable in Trento, but he was after all a police officer. *Vini prestigiosi* was printed on the façade following the name of the firm. Their prestigious wines! I'll never buy a bottle, I thought to myself.

Villa Barbara in Asolo has an exquisite exterior architecture and the interior more than equals its promise. I continued through the Venetian landscape and carefully made my way past dozens of cyclists. The church bells tolled their E-D-C major scale progression as I passed one *Don Camillo* idyll after the other.

The day after Halloween is called *Tutti i Morti* in Italy – all the dead. I started it by going to San Vito, a neighbouring village to Valdobbiadene. I had previously run into the Miotto distillery by chance. Both brothers happened to be out at the time, but I was welcomed back the following day before noon. That afternoon I went to Conegliano and *Scuola Enologica* together with Luciano and Paola.

Distilleria Scuola Enologica di Conegliano

DISTILLERIA
SCUOLA ENOLOGICA
DI CONEGLIANO
GRAPPA
– GIOVANE –

We were greeted by an exuberant Luciano Brotto who showed us the experimental distillery of the school as well as other resources, such as laboratories, a wine store and vineyards. He was accompanied by Stefano Soligo, head of the research unit of Veneto Agricultura – a regional agency that supports the state run school.

"Our most important mission is to develop new technologies and new methods of grappa production, especially from the Prosecco", said Luciano, responsible for the grappa education of the school and teacher of the sensory analysis course. "The processes in the experimental distillery are run by computers – the youth of today expect it. Values for different grape and grappa varieties are recorded and the process can be monitored

The chapel "Il Tempietto" belonging to Villa Barbara.

Villa Barbaro from around 1560, an outstanding example of 16th century Venetian castle-style architecture.

on the computer screen. The *testa* and *coda* are separated automatically. We can switch between the different methods *a vapore* and *bagnomaria* to visualize the differences. The system is *sotto vuoto* (vacuum based) making the vinaccia start to boil at 80 degrees – which is really quite low." According to Luciano, this yields a greater exchange of aromas.

"How the vinaccia is handled is decisive to the quality of grappa," he continued. "It must smell good, and have a nice consistency. Vinaccia is not a waste product. This is why we are intensely researching storage techniques, as well as how to start and interrupt the fermentation at the right time. Controlling the fermentation is crucial."

"People either love grappa or hate it", said Luciano. "Personally, I want to increase the interest in grappa by developing, changing and adapting it to new target groups". *Grappa 3.19* is Luciano's own invention made at his distillery Centopercento in Giavera del Montello. It is a smoked grappa made from the 3 grapes: Prosecco, Cabernet and Incrocio manzoni, which is then stored for 1 year and distilled with 9 innovative methods. "Grappa 3.19 works best when enjoyed with smoked salmon or with a strawberry in it – like champagne," said Luciano with his tongue-in-cheek and mischievous twinkle in his eye. "In very small quantities in very large glasses."

DIST. CENTOPERCENTO
GRAPPA TORBATA 3.19
– INVECCHIATA –

Scuola Enologica di Conegliano – the world's oldest school for wine making and agriculture dating back to 1850 – also includes an experimental grappa distillery for both educational and commercial purposes. The school has its own grappa label. Luciano Brotto is in charge of educating master distillers.

DISTILLERIA LE CRODE
*GRAPPA DI PROSECCO
– GIOVANE –*

Distilleria Le Crode

The following day I headed for *Sinistra Piave*, the left bank of the river Piave, in search of the Distilleria Le Crode, supposedly situated on a hill to the right when travelling from Valdobbiadene. It was a harsh landscape, sheer cliffs, with a severe climate and unforgiving winters. I made my way along the stone riverbank of the Piave and all of a sudden I saw Grappa Le Crode, written in Hollywood letters on the hillside. This still is the only still in the province of Belluno – well, that is also "a position" I thought as an advertising man while turning back. Missed exits had become a part of this trip. After a small bumpy trip up the hill, I made a tight turn in a small courtyard where the road ended. An old lady stood outside the house. *Buongiorno! Mi scusi, signora. C'è una distilleria qui? Si, certo!* The couple who ran the distillery were not there, but I was invited in. She led me upstairs to the *cantina* and very soon the owners

Lucia Gallina, also seen in the opening of the book's first chapter.

Laura Gallina, the daughter of Lucia, and her husband Frederico Arduini run the distillery.

appeared behind me. Frederico Arduini and Laura Gallina, daughter of the old woman, Lucia Gallina.

When the couple founded Le Crode in 1990, Frederico had no background in grappa making, but plenty of experience in marketing and leadership from his days in the grocery business. "I am no *maestro*, but I know how grappa should taste," he declared. "I rent local skilled craftsmen to run the distillery during the grappa season," he continued. "Our *alambicco* is from the 40's using the *a vapore diretto* method. Our range is mostly traditional *grappa giovane* made of local grapes. We also boast a unique grappa, stored on oak, called Malt & Hop, where we mix malt and hops in vinaccia. One third of the grappa is for export."

Frederico, after all, has his roots in sales and marketing.

I LEFT LE CRODE – the name means "the rocks" – and set a course towards Friuli-Venezia Giulia. There are many roads and not all of them are marked on the map. So, if you think you have missed a turn or fear that you have gone too far, continue straight ahead. You will either run into a sign with the name of the place you are looking for, or you will eventually know for certain that you have driven too far. It is not very wise to turn around and look for a place that you have not passed yet.

Distilleria Pagura

The distillery, located in the middle of the village Castions di Zoppola, is surrounded by beautiful houses. Old winery tools and equipment have been given a new aesthetic purpose at the court entrance. A façade glowed crimson red by a wall of leaves. The entire scene was very Italian. The family business is owned and run by Lindo Paguro and his sisters Gianna and Dora. The distillery itself was born in 1876 under the name Sgnaperie. *Sgnapa* means grappa in Venetian. Schnapps! Gianna and Dora gave me a guided tour. The distillery had a distinctly rural charm. The four cooking vessels *caldaie* were cast in wood, which exaggerated the cosy atmosphere. The still is from the 50's and uses the *vapore diretto* method, typical to the region. The shimmering store, *la cantina*, was absolutely charming.

Pagura manufactures traditional, artisan-style grappa using local grapes such as Muscat, Cabernet, Pinot, Verduzzo, Merzemino, Ucelut and Sciaglia. However, the bottles are not at all traditional. Apart from *grappa monovitigno* and *tradizionale* you will also find their *grappa d'Artista*, offered in fantastic glass and ceramic creations. One of the

DISTILLERIA PAGURA
GRAPPA FRIULANA
– GIOVANE –

Distilleria Pagura in Castions di Zoppola, Friuli.

The enchanting "cantina" and Dora Pagura.

Rural charm.

DISTILLERIA PAGURA
GRAPPA
"PER OVE BOUDIN"
– GIOVANE –

designers is Angelo Toppazzini, who is married to Dora Pagura. Angelo invited me with a whistle down to the studio. He picked a bottle from a shelf and wrote my name in elegant handwriting on the label. Another speciality of Pagura.

IT HAD GOTTEN DARK OUTSIDE and and I asked for the shortest way to the main road. Back on the road again I thought of the bottles of Pagura. It is said that the best grappa is found in the simplest of bottles. I understand the underlying principle: that boutique distilleries do not have the resources for design and marketing that the big ones have. But Pagura, an artisan distillery with a long tradition, in fact uses design as a method to bring out the quality of their grappa. They are Italians, after all. It is about communicating and getting seen and finally, when the bottle is on the table, the design becomes a part of the taste sensation. (No matter how much you want to deny it.)

Two more intended visits to distilleries in Friuli remained: *Ceschia* and *Domenis*. Wise from yesterday's outing to Pagura, I planned to take the autostrada east, but all the same I was sucked into highway 13 towards Udine, which is the obvious choice on the map. After two and a half hours squeezed in-between lorry grilles and cargo doors, I had not travelled more than 100 km

Design as a means of communicating quality grappa.

Designer Angelo Toppazzini naming a bottle.

and my schedule was under threat. I was lucky to have visited Pagura yesterday; all three distilleries in one day would never have worked. Suddenly two policemen signalled me to stop. *Buongiorno, signore. Possiamo vedere il libretto?* Please, may we see the *"libretto"*. "Um, I am looking for *Distilleria Ceschia*," was my attempt to divert attention. "Do you know it?" They did. Meanwhile, I looked through insurance papers, service receipts and car inspection papers. Yes, the policemen enjoyed grappa too. *"Il libretto, per favore"* they repeated. Eventually I had to admit that I did not have one. "We don't have those in Sweden". What to do? *Niente.* "Nothing, but it is your obligation as driver to carry one in the car", they said. *Il libretto.* A small booklet, a document, perhaps. I had completely overseen this in my planning. One is also supposed to be carrying a fluorescent vest as well. But the worst was yet to come. I asked to take their picture! *Un'altra volta…* another time… Where do these moronic ideas come from? Probably after near-death experiences.

The two improvised grappa visits of the day ended up being quite summary:

Distilleria Ceschia

Established in 1886, Distilleria Ceschia in Nimis is modern but also the oldest distillery in Friuli. I met Alessandro Ceschia, who runs the company together with his two siblings. Production is based on craftsmanship and technique with *alambicchi* from the late 1940's. *Ceschia*, like so many stills in this region, was destroyed during the Second World War. The method is batchwise distilling, *discontinuo a vapore*. The separation of *cuore* is done automatically, and based on the alcohol strength. The production was not operational during my short visit and I had no opportunity to get a closer look at the installation.

"We make the best grappa in Italy," said Alessandro without hesitation. "Small quantities, high quality and a medium-high price. The only imaginable condition. We produce grappa and various distillates of grapes and fruits. For grappa we use exclusively the yellow Verduzzo grape from Ramandolo in the wine district Colli Orientali." According to

DISTILLERIA CESCHIA
GRAPPA CLASSICA GENTILE
DI RAMANDOLO
– GIOVANE –

Distilleria Ceschia in Nimis, Friuli.

Maestro Alessandro Ceschia holding up a grappa Classica, white and strong. Ceschia stores in steel vats only.

Colli Orientale – the wine district surrounding Distilleria Domenis.

Emilio Domenis in the shop.

Alessandro, the colour of the grape really does not matter. It is the aroma that counts. Their famous grappa *Classica*, presented in a raffia covered bottle, is stored for at least three years and has an alcohol strength of 50 percent. *Gentile* is a milder version and the third variety is very old – from 1971. "Only steel vats are used," said Alessandro. "Oak barrels give a Cognac character that doesn't belong in a grappa."

Distilleria Domenis

Distilleria Domenis is situated close to the city Cividale, in Colli Orientale del Friuli close to Collio, both famous wine districts. I found the distillery outside the town in the middle of the wine fields. The site looked very rational and efficient. The company dates from 1898 and is still owned by the founding family. I met Emilio Domenis who is one of the five part owners, who include his sister and his father. The production is batchwise *discontinuo a vapore* with traditional equipment. The quality of the grappa is guaranteed using computers. Emilio regretted that cameras were not allowed in the distillery.

Well-known grappas from the Domenis are *Storica* and *Blanc e Neri*. Both series contain both grappa *giovane* and *invecchiata*. The young grappas *Storica Nera*, *Storica*, and *Secolo Domenis* – the highest quality – have 50, 50 and 60 percent alcohol respectively. All the vinaccia is sourced from vineyards in Colli Orientale del Friuli and Collio. A speciality is their *kosher grappa* made from vinaccia from kosher wine, distilled by local Jewish wine growers at the Domenis. Another speciality is organic grappa made from the skins of organically grown grapes that are vinificated according to certain purity laws.

DIST. DOMENIS
GRAPPA BLANC E NERI SAUVIGNON BLANC
– GIOVANE –

DUSK WAS DESCENDING as I left Cividale and at Udine I suspected a problem with keeping on track through the town. While my head was spinning like a fighter pilot's, I came up with the simple solution. Follow the trucks! They are usually heading straight through town. I continued my night time navigating and finally found Valdobbiadene. Sometimes you suddenly find yourself travelling on a desolate road with lonely strange house and black windows. Am I on the right track? Am I lost? But it is a part of this kind of travelling. Paola and Luciano were in the kitchen when I got out of the car. "You look tired!" they said. I had driven 350 km. The day before I had covered 180 km – which is quite a trek in north eastern Italy.

On Saturday two new guests arrived at the agriturismo, a secretive military pilot and an ebullient musician. They served the hosts and me a genuine Italian lunch, where the conversation is always as important as the food. *Pasta farfalla* with cheese and broccoli, followed by olives, boiled paprika and finally coffee and a *digestivo*. A Pilzer *grappa giovane* from my mobile and constantly growing collection was demanded. As a final treat a bit of cheese from Naples, the home of the mysterious airman who refused to discuss his profession but was very talkative about all other subjects. The lunch finished at around 5PM, and so was I. I went down for the count on my bed in my room. I woke up a few hours later, worked a bit and then went down to the fridge to have a nibble. There, preparations for the Sunday lunch were in full motion. The pilot was

Somewhere.

The village of San Vito, a close neighbour of Valdobbiadene. Note the sign in the upper left corner that announces a Miotto distillery. I missed it though.

cutting aubergines, frying garlic in oil, and invited me to taste. "How about lunch tomorrow?" he offered.

Sunday started off with a proper breakfast, with boiled eggs from the farm, chestnut honey and *Caffè napolitano*: Pour a cup of strong coffee into the espresso maker without compressing it. Fill it up to the rim only and make a little hole in the middle. Pour in more coffee and make a new hole. Continue until the coffee creates the top. Screw on the top. Sweeten with chestnut honey, preferably in the boiler. All according to the pilot's checklist.

Later Paola helped me to interpret the recordings from the school in Conegliano where all communication had been in Italian, in *tempo presto*, very fast in musical terms. The airman and the violin player arrived at quarter to one and Paola started to set the table. First a pasta with aubergine, and then a piquant *kraut*, together with yesterday's *spumante* and Clinto wine – and above all an animated conversation. I had arranged my grappa collection on one of the kitchen shelves and we tried a few with the coffee. A good grappa should not burn in your throat, said the pilot. It may burn on your tongue, but not in your throat. And unlike wine, grappa shall bubble a little bit when you pour it. We were done at around five o'clock. I wanted to know more about the bubbles when you pour, but was too tired to ask. A pilot and a violin player. Another strange coincidence. I like planes and music. You are on the right path, I heard myself saying.

Monday and I was still in Veneto. Blue sky and a beautiful autumn; Debussy was in the air. The solitude awakens slumbering feelings and images.

I met people all the time but I was still alone. A strange thought occurred to me: I was making two parallel journeys, one external, forward in time, and one internal, backwards in history. The brown bed, the brown windows, the yellow walls – at least in dusky light – sent me back to Christmas 1974 when I had signed up on my first ship, *m/v Sunnanland/SIHV.* The interior of my first flat appeared as if on a photograph. Even old thoughts and moods came over me at times. I thought of Beethoven; to compose one piano sonata, sure, but to compose 32 completely different! In the beginning of the trip, the loneliness had been more acute and I was infected by homesickness, and work was a way to overcome it.

The high point of the trip had been reached. I was convinced of it. In less than a month I had learned more about grappa and met more distillers and people than I had ever dared to hope. Better grappa could hardly be found. My laptop was filled with facts and pictures for an entire book. I could not ask for more. And how much longer would fortune guide me and arrange all these coincidences? But Lombardy, Piemonte, Liguria and Tuscany remained. I still wanted to cross them, if only to get a glimpse of The Last Supper in Milan, visit the Stradivari museum in Cremona or feel the playful breeze of San Remo.

Three nights I intended to spend in Valdobbiadene turned into eleven. The last evening, Paola and Luciano, together with their daughter Anna, brought a *panettone* – Christmas cake – sparkling *spumante* and grappa. They stayed until late and I thanked Paola again for their help in decoding the tape recordings. *"In bocca al lupo!"* she said which means "Good luck!" To this one should reply *"Crepi il lupo!"* Kill the Wolf! But I did not know it then. "With your book project, you have placed yourself in the jaws of the wolf" Paola explained.

The time had come to go west! The next morning my car was packed and I was consulting my map behind the wheel. My cell phone beeped a text message: "Bob Dylan is in your area. Milan 12th and Bologna 10th." I decided to think it over during the next few miles. If I see Dylan in Milan, the journey follows the right course but with an undesired delay. If I meet him in Bologna, my route is completely altered. But change creates energy. I decided to let Dylan lead me. The sun sparkled and the countryside glowed. Debussy was gone, replaced by Dylan, the Beatles, Donovan, the Byrds and the summers of the late 60's. I was heading for Brescia to make a detour to a suitable distillery. A police car was parked along the road. I still did not have a *libretto* but I was the owner of a brand new, garish yellow, fluorescent vest.

I turned away from Brescia and headed for Gussano roaming the countryside without finding the distillery I had in mind. My spirits sank gradually and I set a course for today's destination – Cremona – on the road to Bologna. Stradivari will not fail me. As soon as I found the road, my car was shrouded in *nebbia* – the fog – and the sun and all the colours disappeared. *Incrocio pericoloso* flashed a road sign – even warning texts sound beautiful in Italian. Dangerous intersection. I could only see a small portion of the road in front of me. Where was I going? What was I doing here? I was driving as in a tunnel, far away from home. Music was my travel companion and the singers had become my intimate friends, friends that encouraged me to continue through the fog.

Cremona was colourless and strange, and lured me into its *centro storico* only to toy with me for a while. When I managed to get rid of the car, I asked for the tourist information and was directed to the info centre for the town. Not the same thing. It happened to be close to the tourist information though. I got a tip for a central hotel and checked in without further ado. I was numb after my grey journey and the hustle and bustle of the city. A sort of Christmas mood had started to grow in the shops. The fact that it was only the second week of November did not bother me at all. That was not the issue. I just did not want any Christmas mood at all. The clerk at the hotel suggested restaurant *Duomo* where I enjoyed a saffron coloured *carbonara* with a glass of red wine. *Cemeriere, un caffè e una grappa, per favore.* So, it is from Piemonte! *Buonissima*! Perhaps there are new peak sensations ahead after all?

Cremona was an emergency landing with poor visibility. In the morning I looked up the town museum and the Stradivari exhibition. I was told that no original instruments were here. So what – violins look pretty all the same, and they are not being played within their glass boxes. I watched a video about Stradivari in an empty room. The film was accompanied by a violin concerto by Bach. I wondered if they played better during Bach's time? Most would probably disagree. Do they play better now than Paganini? What does "play better" mean? What does "taste good" mean? Anyway, the thought that they would have played worse when the music was current feels absurd in a sense.

I drove towards Bologna with the computer on top volume. The music that had left me unmoved on the banks of Lake Garda was now taking hold of me. Just like with grappa – the resistance was no more and I could read the code. The message was understood.

I found Bologna's central station with little difficulty (I had been there just last spring) and went to the tobacconist shop that I knew would sell tickets to the Dylan concert. I got a seat in *Tribuna A*. It was a bad seat. Far back in the temporary bleachers. I jumped down and manoevred to get to the front of the stage when the show began. I wondered: is Bob pulling my leg? His voice was ruined from too many years on the road touring. It had two levels that he leapt between: a low talking mood and a high-pitched scream. Every phrase ended high up there. His singing made no sense really. And no guitar. He played some

Cremona – the city of Antonio Stradivari (1644-1737), the wizard among all violin makers.

sensitive harmonica solos – his former furious blowing was now transferred into his singing. His song and harmonica are his fantastic orchestra that can express everything, but only he can hear it. "I can't be like I was before" or something similar he sang. People were smoking around me and taking photos. An attendant cleared his way through the crowd, gave a roar and disappeared. People were smoking and taking photos. The camera diodes glowed like lit cigarettes all around me.

My stay in Bologna was hectic and I was tired of driving and at night navigating. I looked forward to settling in for a few days in Tuscany and catching up on my notes and recovering. On the road south I felt I was reaching the apogee. The ties to my home were stretched to the point of bursting. The weather was grey but without *nebbia* and the milky white light reminded me of Easter in Sweden. I was running out of oxygen. The piano solo from the computer was refreshing like the spring water of the Dolomites. Once again, the music pushed me, like it did on my misty approach to Cremona. You are here and now, I thought to myself. You are travelling, this is your life at the moment. Where you'll end up really doesn't matter. You have time. Keep on.

TUSCANY

With the Tuscan mountains came blue skies and a rebirth of summer. I wound in and out of tunnels and over bridges, high above the green valleys. It felt like flying. I like it when tunnels are sloping downwards – in case of engine failure. I spied Florence in the distance. Nice to just drive on by! I had not set any final destination for the day, but I wanted to pass Greve di Chianti where a few stills are supposed to be. The car ate the miles as I headed down the freeway towards Rome. I took the exit at San Giovanni, unfortunately a little too far south. I asked a man in the tollbooth

1. Florence
2. Greve in Chiar
3. Siena
4. Montepulcian
5. Montalcino
6. Paganico
7. Pitigliano
8. Saturnia
9. Grosseto
10. Livorno
11. Pisa
12. Carrara

to direct me to Greve in Chianti. He nodded and told me to head to the right and follow the road signs. It can not be that simple. And it was not. After a few uncertain kilometres, I passed a wine shop – *enoteca* – but did not turn around until I reached the next village, Bucine. I was strongly in need of guidance.
I returned to the wine shop where the owner was unloading boxes from a car when I pulled up, map in hand. He shook his head confirming that the minor roads are always troublesome. And the road I had been sent on was actually closed right at the moment. He directed me north on the motorway. "Not again!" I sighed in silence. Luckily I happened to mention the purpose of my trip before I drove off. "Come on in," he said and showed me the grappas he had in stock. "There aren't any distilleries of note in Tuscany anyway." He only had one Tuscan grappa on the shelves. It was made in Friuli.

We looked at my list of distilleries and I placed a finger on *Bonollo* – Italy's largest industrial grappa producer with several factory-style distilleries. He shook his head. *Distilleria D.E.T.A* then? "No, that is also an industrial producer. However, there is a distillery that makes boutique grappa not very far from here." He told me to drive to Siena and then towards Grosseto and take the exit near Civitella Marittima. And in Aratrice you will find it – *Distilleria Nannoni*.

The sun was shining with all its might, it felt like summer and I was on my way to a recommended distillery. It had become something of a rule of thumb – to only visit advised distilleries. I found the exit from the highway without any problems and I stopped at a service station. I decided to ask directions at once. Nobody there. I continued on my way, following the winding road down into the valley, but I never discovered the final lead. I ended up in a village perched on a hill in the distance, where I asked an old man. "Turn around and then right after a few kilometres" he told me. I went down again and landed in the beautiful summer landscape and soon I detected the sign saying Aratrice. I followed the little road over the fields towards a pillar of smoke pointing to the sky like an apostrophe sign in the autumn scenery. As dusk approached later, the picture reminded me of Sweden.

The large gate to the distillery was closed. As I sauntered around I sensed the shape of a grand manor house and I heard a dog barking. A farmer stood tinkering in a shed close by. "*Certo*, he replied, the distillery is open. Just ring the doorbell." I rang and through the squeaking of the loudspeaker I heard a young female voice. I delivered my standard phrases, to which she replied in English "I'm coming!" I was met with a huge beaming smile and an aura, almost palpable.

Distilleria Nannoni

Priscilla Occhipinti showed me around. Production was in full swing. She was very animated. Nannoni was established in 1975 by *maestro*

Cascate del Gorello. The constantly warm and sulphurous waterfall in Saturnia.

Gioacchino Nannoni who wanted to create a new style of grappa made from vinaccia from the famous Brunello grape of Tuscany. In this way *winery grappa* was born and together with other innovations – most prominent being Nonino's *grappa monovitigno* – they contributed to the upswing in the popularity of grappa.

Three women currently own and manage Nannoni: Priscilla Occhipinti, Morena Orlandini and Rossana Rossini. Priscilla, an enologist educated at Florence University, runs the still. She started as an apprentice with Gioacchino in 1997 and has kept his methods and passion for grappa alive. She also teaches grappa techniques at the university and organisations like *F.I.S.A.R. – Federazione Italiana Sommelier Albergatori Ristoratori*. Morena and Rossana take care of bottling, customer contact and so on.

The still *a metodo discontinuo a vapore diretto* was constructed and built by Gioacchino Nannoni. "The *alambicco* is my copper orchestra," said Priscilla. "It changes constantly and I have to change with it. Gioacchino taught me to listen to all the instruments and how to keep the equipment finely tuned with a soldering iron. All the instruments

DIST. NANNONI
GRAPPA DI BRUNELLO DA SIGARO TOSCANA
– RISERVA –

Distilleria Nannoni behind the gates.

The young maestra Priscilla Occhipinti.

"Fresh raw material above all".

"Distillation is heavy work. Distilleries that show pictures of women shovelling vinaccia are not real distilleries – they are the ones that buy grappa from genuine distilleries and bottle it," says Priscilla Occhipinti.

DIST. NANNONI
GRAPPA DI BRUNELLO
ORO DEI CARATI
— RISERVA —

of the *alambicco* are equally important to the harmony of a grappa; for balance between the aroma, taste and colour. As the equipment changes so does the grappa. You can't do the same grappa twice." I came to think of the ancient philospher Herclitus' words *Panta rei* – everything flows. You cannot step into the same river twice, he also wrote.

Nannoni mainly produces grappa for wineries. The vinaccia is collected from the wineries and the grappa is distilled, stored in wooden barrels, bottled and branded with the winery's label. The name Nannoni is only in the fine print. Only a few grappas are sold under Nannoni's own label, such as grappa *di Sigaro Toscano* and *Oro dei carati*.

"The round aroma from these Brunello grappas comes from the oak barrels that have been used for storing wine," said Priscilla, "That way the wine makers passion shines through into the grappa."

The short distillation season from September to November is intense. The *alambicco* never cools. Priscilla collects the boxes of vinaccia from the wine makers, drives a loader between the raw material storehouse and the boiler, and at the same time supervises the distilling process. She also keeps the fire stoked with used vinaccia. Everything is

In Sweden?

A Chianti Classico wine producer getting his grappa made.

recycled. The grape skins become energy, the seeds are sent away for processing and the waste products from the distilling process are used as raw products by chemical companies.

"The art of distilling is not about how to separate out the methyl alcohol but to create a taste sensation," explained Priscilla. "The *cuore* is present when the alcohol content is between 85 and 50 percent, but the truly superb grappa is to be found between 80 and 68 percent – *that* I have to smell and taste. And those tiny flies, the *moscerini*, on the *bacinella* (glass bowl with the alcohol meter), signify that a good grappa is flowing. They are true connoisseurs."

"Mostly, we use red vinaccia even though the colour of the grape is not as important as the freshness. The vinaccia must be used within three days of arrival. The decomposition process starts immediately and after a little while it begins to smell bad, get mouldy and the grape's character disappears. Still, some producers will put grappa "Moscato" or "Brunello" on the label even though none of the grape's aroma is left. Some industrial-style grappa makers produces an almost clean spirit that is then flavoured with sugar and aromatic additives. Some even have small *alambicco discontinuo* which they use as a demonstration model for the visitors only.

"Vinaccia constitutes not only the beginning but also the end of the grappa. Grappa should remind you of vinaccia, your thoughts should connect with the grape," said Priscilla. She often tastes the grappa by hand like a perfume with a few drops on her palms. With her hands cupped together she breathes in the aroma through her nose. "Grappa is meditation," she said. "I look for an impression, for the pictures that grappa stir in me. Time is important. Not until the grappa is poured into the glass the aromas start to build. I can let different grappas stand for hours and then taste them one after the other to see how the tastes and aromas develop."

"Grappa tastes best at an alcohol content of 40-45 percent. Strength is not a barrier in itself but too much binds the flavour. An undiluted grappa direct from the *alambicco* doesn't have much flavour but when water is added the aromas burst out."

"You were lucky to arrive right now," she said. "We are running out of vinaccia – one week later and I wouldn't be distilling any longer." Thank you Bob Dylan for taking me this way, I thought to myself. I mean, what were the odds that I would have come across Nannoni, if I had come a few weeks later and from an entirely different direction?

Gioacchino Nannoni

"I knew that Tuscany had enormous potential, with its rich source of vinaccia. Here they produce Chianti, Brunello and Nobile – wonderful wines, rich in tannins and inebriating aromas. Here a truly great grappa could be born – a winery grappa that could tell the tale of Tuscany."

I visited the vineyards and saw the grapes being harvested, but something was missing. Veneration. I knew the sacred respect that the Piemontese farmers had shown the vinaccia, which was then delivered on silver trays to the distilleries. But here in Tuscany, the grape skins lay exposed to the sun in the courtyard to be scratched at by the chickens.

Today, I am proud of Tuscany's wine makers – they produce beautiful wines as well as good vinaccia. It demonstrates my belief that those who treat vinaccia disrespectfully cannot produce a good wine."

Gioacchino Nannoni was born on the 29th of February 1936 in Florence and died on the 11th of August 2007 in Grosseto.

I left Distilleria Nannoni in the afternoon and went westwards to intercept the motorway north of Grosseto. I had reached the most southern point of my trip and was now turning back. A soft and beautiful Saturday afternoon light settled over the landscape as I drove tired and still bloated after a lunch of Tuscan specialities in Civitella Marittima. I had had everything; *antipasto*, *primo* and *secondo piatto* as well as *dolce* and *caffè* – with a mouthful of grappa, of course, served to myself and the distiller herself by the head waiter. I opened up the computer beside me and selected a piano concerto by Mozart. I needed a hearty dose of crystal clear scales to cheer me up but at the same time calm me down. It helped, because even with the handwritten directions on my lap I was not really certain of where I was, until I spied the coastline in the distance. There are no simple directions in Italy.

By the time I arrived in Pisa it was pitch black. No tower was in sight. Another late night in a strange city. Now, where was I going to stay? In the fringes of the bigger cities there are always plenty of hotels of both unreasonable and reasonable prices. The problem is finding one of the latter in the dark of night. Despite this I began my search in the central roundabout and soon a saw a signpost decorated with at least five star-rated hotel arrows. I chose to follow the signpost of one of the hotels with fewer stars, a hunt which led me out of town. Good, I thought to myself, the further I am out of town the more reasonable it will be. I ended up in the suburbs beside a lifeless service apartment complex, where I turned around and headed out onto the "main road" with overhead lighting, service stations and probably a motel. A bigger hotel caught my attention and I quickly stepped out of the vehicle and into the lobby. "Four stars" added the nice woman at the reception desk after telling me the price. "A little bit over my travel budget", I tried. (That's a savvy reply, to suggest that it is over your travel allowance – as if you are breaking some kind of law by accepting it. A pleasant way of bargaining, although she was not influenced by it.) So I checked in, relieved after all. The room was nice and what does the price matter for one night. Especially bearing in mind what I had

The leaning tower?

been offered so far: lunches, dinners, grappa and even rooms for the night but in particular the amiability and all the wonderful things I had experienced. It is really weird how we sometimes completely misjudge proportions of things. Besides I was still full from lunch and at the same time drained of all my energy. I flopped onto the bed, called my wife before prostrating myself for a couple of hours in front of the TV in a semi-coma. Then I went up and wrote down yesterdays' events.

The breakfast buffet was a good assortment and at the table I contemplated the differences between this and previous hotels from my journey. Here, all the guests were international. The atmosphere had a distinct feeling of "like home, even when you are travelling." The personnel were not unfriendly, they were proper but a vague sense of snootiness was not too far away. I thought about Zaccaria in Bassano del Grappa with his happy greeting of *buongiorno il professore!* Though I did not understand many of the following words, I could feel what was meant. It is like what the Swedish actor Per Oscarsson once said to a director who complained that he was not articulating clearly enough in an emotional scene. "Well at least one can hear that I am bloody angry!"

Here I was in Pisa, the sun was shining invitingly and I wondered where I should be leaning – to the tower of course! One of the world's most famous buildings, right in the middle of *centro storico*. A traffic and parking nightmare in other words. Incredibly, I found an available parking spot on a little *piazza* by the river. A local passer-by informed me "Yes, of course you can park here, no charge today." When I had seen and photographed the tower from all angles I returned to the car and chivalrously offered the parking spot to a French family. That was when a police officer showed up and shooed both of us away. It goes to show that you cannot always trust what people tell you, even if you ask in your best school-grade Italian.

Now I had seen it. Even as I child I had a picture of this magical tower in my brain. Now I had seen it in reality. Now that magic image was gone.

LIGURIA

I took the Via Aurelia out of Pisa towards Genoa. The Via Aurelia is the old road that hugs the whole coastline of Liguria. But if you want to travel fast, take the *autostrada* which runs higher up and further inland but in a straight line.
I took a detour to the marble mines in Carrara. The mountain actually shimmers. Pretty soon I arrived in the town of La Spezia, but its glamour did not attract me and I continued on the Via Aurelia that immediately started to climb and wind into the mountains. I started to think "where am I going to sleep tonight?"
I turned and went back to the town, stopped and contemplated at a signpost saying Cinque Terre.

1. La Spezia
2. Cinque Terre
3. Ne
4. Chiavari
5. Portofino
6. Sori
7. Genoa
8. San Remo
9. Ventimiglia

Portofino, almost like a picture.

I was homeless, hungry and irresolute – not a great combination. I dropped the seaside idyll and hit the *autostrada* and was immediately rewarded with a road sign "Service station 1500m." After my stop, like a new person I headed out on the highway again in that late afternoon daylight. At Sestri Levante I left the motorway and descended to the Aurelia again, to the towns and the possible lodgings. There are no small towns in this part of Italy. Even if on the map they seem like insignificant dots, in reality they are magnificent Riviera towns in colonial style with beach promenades, palm trees and white yachts. I passed through Cavi and made a serious attempt to find a hotel in Chiavari but ended up in the *centro storico*. The price was all right but the location was too tight and tricky. On second thought I did not want to stay in a city. I needed a few days to catch up on my writing and regain strength.

    With the evening the contours became increasingly blurred and I drove with my senses on high beam. Every signpost made me pause – a hotel? A pension? A room? Often the signs flashed by so suddenly I was forced to backtrack to examine them more closely. It may take a quite a while before you find a turning space on the narrow road. I drove through Zoagli without success but on the downward slope towards Sori I noticed a brightly lit sign on my left – Bed & Breakfast. Not until after the bridge downtown did I find a spot where I could cheekily manoeuvre the car into the opposite direction. You take your life in your hands. I stopped in front of the friendly lit sign, stepped through the ironwork gate and rang the doorbell. An older gentleman opened the door and presently he interrupted my fumbled Italian with perfect English. "Certainly, I have a room available," he replied. The room was on the upper floor. The atmosphere was airy, neat and inviting. A balcony door. I could sense the presence of the Mediterranean. This was definitely somewhere I could stay a few days. I gladly paid my host in advance.

    "I am too old for grappa" he commented on my mission in Italy and gave me a map and some restaurant tips. Tired and hungry after my journey on the Via Aurelia, I walked down the road to the bridge and church. The church spire

Carrara and its marvel, the marble.

rose like an apparition by the beach. Green church bells in a light blue belfry! The restaurant *Vintage* was close and I asked for a beer at once and ordered just a *secondo piatto* – a slice of veal and a glass of red wine: *Nostrano, per favore.* I sat there thinking about my family and children – I was the only guest I suppose – and I enjoyed the meal and Chet Baker's trumpet in the background; the atmosphere was decidedly muted. I wondered about Piemonte grappa.

A *salvaging sign for the late traveller.*

The city of Sori near Genoa.

Could it exceed what I had experienced so far? I asked the *cameriere* (the waiter) to recommend a grappa from Piemonte and very soon realized that new taste experiences were still awaiting me.

When I put the key in the door of the pension *Villa Castagnola*, I discovered four new guests – two couples from Kentucky on a road trip through Europe with Florence as their final destination. We spoke for a moment until it became obvious that one of the gentlemen in the group was a little sour. His mouth took a decided downturn when I told him about my trip. "He is the only driver among us and has just quit smoking," explained the others after he had gone to bed. What a bad timing, I thought.

I continued my conversation with the exuberant Americans though the driver stayed in his room. "Most Americans probably regard Europe as a place of their roots, a place one really wants to go," I said – and released a roar of laughter. "You don't say" they replied and told me about a conversation they

Typical Genoa style houses with painted façades. The church Parrocchiale in Sori is also colourful.

The Sori moon.

had with a friend before the trip. The young man wondered how they were getting to Europe. "Are you driving", he asked.

    The next morning I went out onto the balcony and photographed the Mediterranean before I flipped open the laptop at the breakfast table and continued writing. I asked one of the staff about pizzerias and she made a few phone calls. She told me that restaurants are usually closed on Mondays, and furthermore it was low season now. But *Al Boschetto* was open and it was only a 20 minute walk away. That evening I took my bag, and a flashlight and set off down the road. In a curve of the road I spied a green neon light. *Al Boschetto* is split in two: *il ristorante* on the right side and *la focacceria* on the left.

I stepped into the warmth of the *focacceria* and ordered a pizza and carafe of red wine. What a wonderful wine! Thick as blood. I had not eaten since breakfast. The pizza arrived glowing white with mozzarella, very large and thin. A *focaccia* of course, the thin bread! Just like the ones my family had in Riquewhir I thought and remembered a journey we made to Alsace when our children were not quite grown up. I also thought about a trip to Sorrento – even if the pizza is thicker there. Oh my God, here I am sitting alone, drinking wine in a restaurant in Liguria, by a winding road and up there, somewhere, a motorway runs through the mountain. The grappa in my hand is an explosion of flowers – a *Moscato del Piemonte* from *Distillerie Francoli*. Like honey almost.

I spoke to the bartender about grappa on my way out. He gave me a newspaper that had grappa as a topic and mentioned that there is only one still in Liguria. *Distilleria Portofino* just outside of Chiavari, in Ne. As I left the restaurant it was raining but it did not bother me. *The best grappa is made in autumn.* Back in my pension I grabbed my camera and went out again and shot the Sori moon.

DIST. PORTOFINO
*GRAPPA DI VERMENTINO LIGURE
– INVECCHIATA –*

Distilleria Portofino

The following day I rang Anticha distilleria di Portofino, also called Fratelli Parma, and booked an appointment for the afternoon. I left at around half past two with only a breakfast in my stomach and found the distillery with relatively little trouble just four kilometres outside of Chiavare. I ran into the son, Simone Parma, on a pile of vinaccia with a pitchfork in his hand. *"Mi scusi"* I said and then apologised for my lateness. I had only just met his father who was not too happy because he had expected me at two o'clock. "No, no, no problem," said Simone, inviting me in and introduced me to the *alambicco a metodo discontinuo a vapore diretto*. I recognised the shiny column. "It is the same as Pilzer in Faver has," I said. Simone raised his eyebrows.

"We are the only distillery in Liguria and our vinaccia comes from the regions renowned vineyards like Vermentino, Pigato, Rossese and Cinque Terre," said Simone. His father started the distillery in 1963 and tradition is very important to Simone who runs the business today. He is not enticed by modern trends and instead produces grappa like it should taste, preferably from a single grape variety, *grappa monovitigno*. I did not understand everything he said but his commitment and passion could not be misinterpreted. He reminded me of Priscilla Occhipinti in Tuscany. Both fiery souls. Young. Timely. *I maestri del futuro* – the grappa masters of the future.

DIST. PORTOFINO
*GRAPPA DI SCIACCHETRÀ DELLE CINQUE TERRE
– RISERVA –*

The young maestro Simone Parma of Distilleria Portofino.

I TOOK THE AUTOSTRADA BACK – I was hungry – and chose the *uscita* (exit) Recco and then straight to the pension and a shower. I grabbed my bag and torch and strolled downtown towards *Al Boschetto* but noticed a sign saying *Edobar Trattoria*. I decided to followe the arrow and found a restaurant a hundred metres along, brightly lit up and welcoming. A rustic Italian *trattoria* and *pizzeria* with red and white chequered tablecloths, brown chairs and a genuine atmosphere. "*Una birra piccola e il menù, per favore*" I said. (A small beer and the menu, please.) As antipasto I ordered a *panissa* – a traditional Ligurian dish made of chickpeas and olive oil among other ingredients – "and as *primo piatto: gnocchi al pesto*. And an *insalata mista*, a mixed salad, a glass of wine, and water, *frizzante* sparkling. *E come secondo piatto vorrei…*" but I was interrupted by the waiter who knew I would not manage that much. The finishing grappa, a *Prosecco* from *Distilleria Bonaventura Maschio* in Veneto, smelled of vinaccia and I liked it.

The olive oil and especially the red wine vinegar also tasted vinaccia. I thought of my first uncertain encounter with vinaccia in Trentino and how that flavour had now changed into something good, something I would look for in a grappa. "The dregs" is really not a proper English word for vinaccia, at least not fresh vinaccia. It might possibly work as a description of the raw product one would find in the huge storage containers of some big industry distilleries.

In Piazza Vittorio Alfieri you will find your way.

The Cathedral of Asti built in the 14th century on the ruins of a previous Romanesque church.

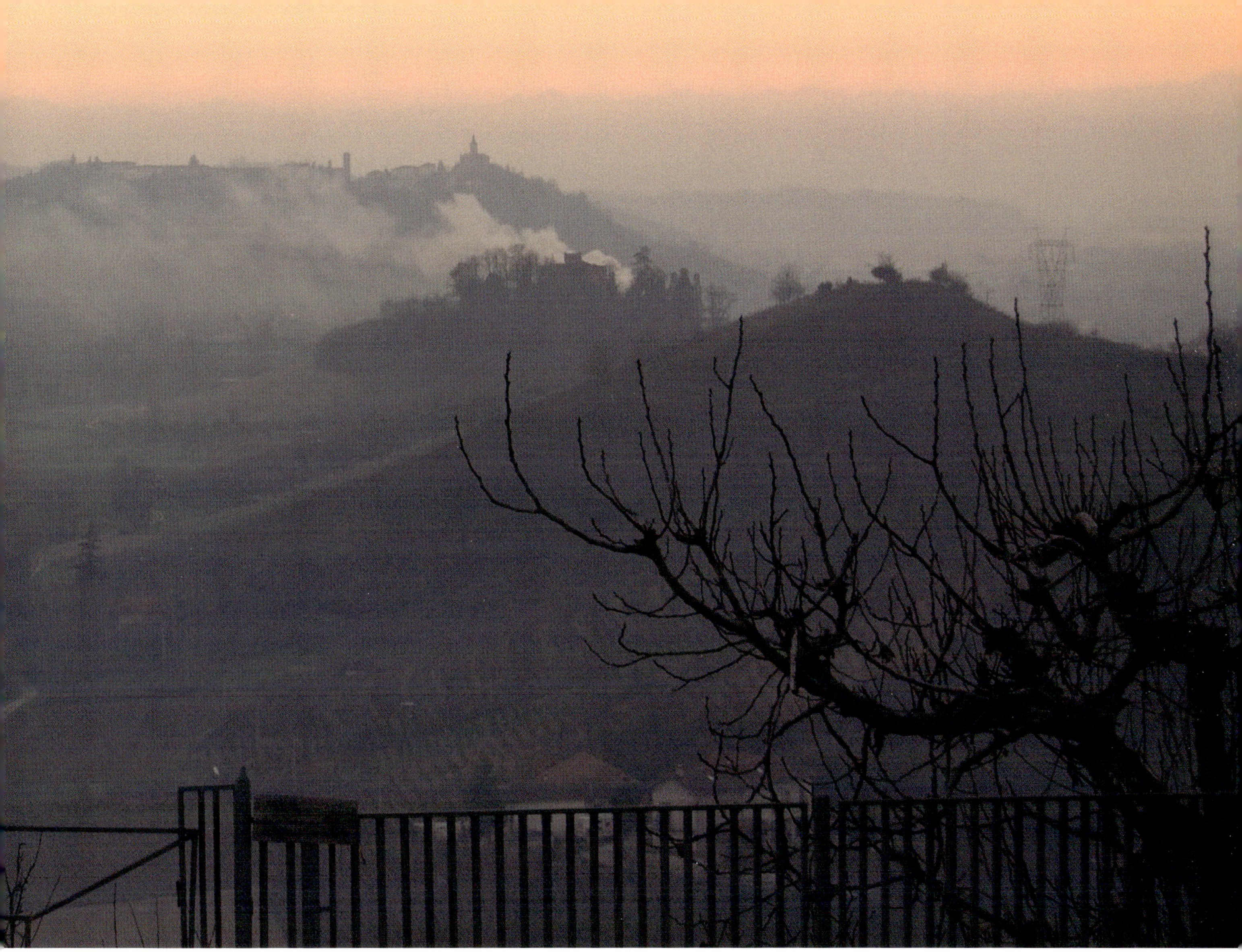

PIEMONTE

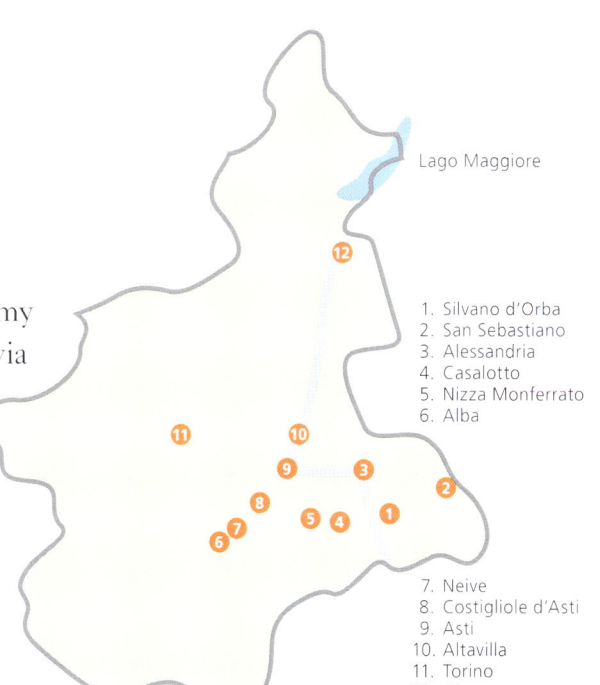

THE FOLLOWING DAY I devoted to catching up on my notes and planning the drive to Piemonte: to Asti via Genoa and Alessandria. I left Sori at around eleven heading south on to the *autostrada* that by and by led into the lofty system of bridges and tunnels that charmingly hug and perforate the coastline of Genoa. I fixed my mind on the road number A26 and wound up on the north side of the town towards Alessandria and Asti, though

Lago Maggiore
1. Silvano d'Orba
2. San Sebastiano
3. Alessandria
4. Casalotto
5. Nizza Monferrato
6. Alba
7. Neive
8. Costigliole d'Asti
9. Asti
10. Altavilla
11. Torino
12. Ghemme

The yearly truffle festival in San Sebastiano in Val Curone, not very far from Alessandria, takes place in November. Reservations at the restaurants need to be made well in advance, a year or so...

I did not know how. My goal was the *Distilleria Rovero*, which I had pinned on my computer in my lap – on the wrong spot I found out when I was chasing the pointer in the *centro storico* of Asti. Instead I followed the signs towards the tourist information office and parked in the Piazza Vittorio Alfieri. As in Conegliano, the tourist office was extremely helpful. The nice woman inside started by handing me a catalogue of hotels, pensions and *agriturismi*, before fetching a map of the region and circling six distilleries and noting their names, addresses and telephone numbers. I asked about accommodation and she rang an *agriturismo* just outside of town. "It's easy to find" she said, "It's in a village called San Marzanotto on top of a hill." *Perfetto*! Of course one should stay on a hill when in Piemonte!

As I drove into the greenery of the hill, the road started to climb, and I saw a familiar sign pointing left: *Azienda Rovero*. "So that's where the still is," I thought. Since I had time on my hands I turned left with the intention of booking a meeting for the following day. As usual, I cautiously peeked into the distillery trying to unobtrusively get attention, just like at a mechanic's. Production was in full swing. Smoke billowed white from the chimney and the yard steamed with freshly distilled vinaccia. *Maestro* Franco Rovero came out and I presented myself and my purpose. He peered archly at me, took a drag on his cigarette butt, escorted me to the office and called his nephew Enrico, then returned to his *alambicco*. I was telling Enrico about my grappa trip, as best I could, when he all of a sudden invited me to a party. On the very same evening they were holding a dinner for the grape growers that deliver vinaccia. Piemonte was off to a great start I thought and continued my journey up to the farm on the hill.

Near the crest of the hill, the road was divided by a wall that at first glance looked like some sort of fortification. I randomly chose to go left but ended up on

a narrow road that wound its way down the steep vineyards again and I decided to turn back on the spot. The road was not much wider than the car so I had to make a precision turn with only millimetres to spare, otherwise I would have ended up with the back wheels in the cement ditch.

Back on the top I chose the road to the right that continued up a little way before reaching houses but then took an immediate dip into the valley again. After ten meters I stamped on the brake, then reversed back up to the top of the hill, pushed down the clutch and felt a bang under my foot as the pedal slammed the floor. The clutch cable. Luckily there was enough space for cars to pass and thankfully it had not happened two minutes earlier as I was driving on the other narrower road. A crane would have been needed to move the car from that position, or a helicopter more likely. Now there I was, sitting in a car with a broken clutch cable on top of a hill in Piemonte at dusk. I turned on the hazard lights, stepped out and rang the *agriturismo* where I was going to stay. A woman answered with *buongiorno*. I told her my name hastily followed by "*La macchina è rotta,*" (My car has broken down) and she started to laugh and said "Ieh speakeh Englisheh…I can 'elp you. I know a mechanic." She was soon there and loaded my luggage in her car. From the street the *agriturismo I Suri* looked like any other house in San Marzanotto but when I entered the courtyard a *vista* of Piemonte opened up with billowing vineyards in the mist of the twilight.

A lively mechanic picked me up and we drove to my car. He immediately dove to the car floor and started fiddling around, before motioning that he suddenly needed something, a tow truck I presumed. We went to his very elegant house and workshop, situated on top of a hill, of course. We changed cars, a third person joined us and we went back. Yes, this car would probably be capable of towing,

An Italian car repair shop.

I thought. At my car the mechanic jumped out and sat in the drivers seat, started over the engine and yanked the gear shift. "Well, I am a car mechanic, you know" he said, or at least thought, and drove off.

That night with the wine growers at the restaurant *Il Milin* in *Azienda Rovero's agriturismo* was a gastronomic feast with a strain of magic – I happened to be there by pure chance. The menu was composed of Piemonte specialities accompanied by the *Roveros'* own wine and grappa. I was seated at the table with Enrico, his girlfriend Michela and *maestro* Franco who also attended his guests. When the guests had gone, Franco said "There is a grappa seminar in Silvano d'Orba on Saturday. A couple of the local distillers and myself are going to discuss the concept of quality grappa. It has never been done before. Would you like to come along?" I pinched myself. How is this possible? How come I was landing in the right places and moments all the time? It was as if fate had a plan. I did not do anything to make it happen, I hardly made any effort at all – maybe that was why.

My room at the *I Suri* was ice-cold despite the glowing heater. Houses here are built to be cool. It takes a summer sun to warm the stone walls in winter time though. I found a blanket in another room; I was the only guest. I froze but at the same time I did not, thanks to the inner glow of circumstance. I understood that not doing absolutely everything in my power to make this idea of a book become reality was to betray the Gods and life itself, betray everyone and everything I love, betray Italy, the distillers and all the wonderful people I had met during my journey. These were my thoughts that first star-filled night in my cold room on a hill in Piemonte.

I ate a simple breakfast by the arched window with the weakly glowing Caco tree outside. I was still warm from my steaming morning shower. Despite the cold air I had managed to keep myself warm under the layers of covers and blankets. My dreams were as always: strange but not unpleasant. They held the usual collection of characters and occasional newcomers. I took my camera, bag and computer and wandered off down to the distillery and the meeting with *maestro* Franco Rovero. The air was crisp and the light was soft; there was a sort of Christmas feeling over the village.

Romano Levi – the legend

"Good quality raw material, good equipment and good fire are the simple secrets behind good grappa. Plus a burning passion to create it. Passion is what gets me out of bed every morning before the sun rises to prepare for the first batch of the day."

The words are Romano Levi's – the mythical and almost canonised grappa master from Neive in the province of Cuneo, Piemonte. Here he has lived an almost hermit-like existence, like a monk in his monastery, the old distillery that was started by his father in 1925. In 1945, Romano took over the business at only 16 years of age, after his mother was killed in an air-raid. His father had passed away in 1933.

"I never chose grappa as a career; it was circumstance that forced me into it. Grappa chose me and I was captured by it. I am not even a connoisseur, just one of the inmates who is fighting for survival. And to try and do my work the best I can."

The distillery is one of the few of its kind that continues to heat the boiler with an open flame *a fuoco diretto*. The fuel is made from pressed blocks of vinaccia from last years' yield.

The *alambicco* is 80 years old. "A jewel that is as reliable as a Swiss watch," says Romano Levi. *Cuore* is tapped into four wooden vats of varying wood and stored. Ash and chestnut do not affect the colour of the distillate but acacia and oak give it a golden tone. Nevertheless, in the end the four barrels will be blended together. Levi only does one type of grappa. "Regardless of all else, it is the quality of the steam that counts," he says. His grappa is harsh, abrasive and rustic and is said to reflect the origins of grappa, but it becomes extremely elegant after ageing for many years. It is not easy to get a chance to taste it though, because each bottle is unique with an equally unique hand painted label by Romano Levi himself. Thus a masterpiece for collectors and few of them are opened to be drunk.

Romano Levi reveals the secret to Maurizio Fava, a slow-food and grappa expert.

Collectors items.

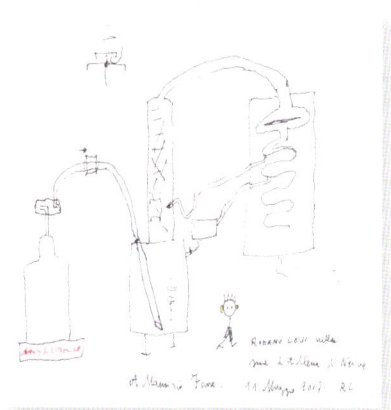

Levi's sketch of the distilling process, dedicated to Maurizio Fava.

Distilleria Rovero

Azienda Rovero was an ordinary farm and winery until 1980 when the owners changed direction, introduced new techniques and starting the grappa production. Barbera is the dominant grape, however Grignolino and other typical grapes of Piemonte are cultivated. Diversity is what differentiates Azienda Rovero from others – they produce wine and distil grappa as well as run a restaurant and an *agriturismo*, all with an eco-friendly agenda. All the wines are made from organically grown grapes. All the grappas made from their own grapes have the organic label – a marketing strategy that attracts ever increasing numbers of customers , especially from Germany and Switzerland.

Rovero also produces grappa for the local grape growers. Only the fine print reveals the origin of the grappa and Rovero as the distillers.

The equipment in the distillery consists of a dual system of independent *bagnomaria a discontinuo*. A batch of 400 kilos of vinaccia takes about two and a half hours to distil and produces around 30 litres of undiluted grappa. The quantity varies according to the level of alcohol in the raw material. The alcohol strength of the finished grappa is somewhere between 41 and 51 percent depending on the grape variety.

DISTILLERIA ROVERO
GRAPPA NEBBIOLO
– GIOVANE –

Franco Rovero, one of the owners in action.

Azienda Rovero: winery, distillery and agriturismo in one, is run by the brothers Franco, Claudio and Michelino Rovero and his son Enrico, including their wives.

All their white grappas are *monovitigno*, in other words they are made from single grape varieties that are stored and distilled separately, and characterizes each grappa and give it its name.

"The freshness of the vinaccia is the most important contributing factor to the quality of a grappa" said *maestro* Franco. "Since we grow and make the wine ourselves we have access to a first-class raw product, but also the vinaccia we buy locally is fresh naturally."

The distillation column has nine plates regulated by valves on the exterior of the column. During grappa production all the plates are utilised, whereas distillates from whole fruits are less demanding and require only a few plates.

The *alambicco* is secured with official seals to prevent any taste testing. Franco Rovero hovered over the equipment with a constant eye on the alcohol meter. As the alcohol strength reached 80 percent he informed me, "It is now time to drain the *cuore* and let the grappa out until the alcohol meter reads around 55 percent. That is when the *coda* starts flowing."

DISTILLERIA ROVERO
GRAPPA DI BARBERA
– RISERVA –

Claudio and Franco waiting for the cuore ...

... to come or quit flowing.

I Surì agriturismo on top of San Marzanotto near Asti. One of many vineyards with B&B service in Piemonte, and everywhere in Italy. Agriturismo are mainly used by Italians and their families. You will not be overcharged.

AT THE AGRITURISMO I opened up the laptop on the breakfast table, anticipated a long Friday evening of work and began downloading the harvest of photos from that day. Then my host appeared and invited me to dinner in the large dining room one floor below. I was instantly glad. She informed me that they usually arrange dinner parties with Piemonte specialities and the theme this weekend was *Novello* wine and *Bagna Caôda*. "I have a few friends downstairs, join them," she said. *Bagna Caôda* is a unique salsa – a blend of olive oil, anchovies and garlic in equal proportions, which is used as a dip for vegetables. The salsa is put in the middle of the table and much like a fondue is kept warm by a tea light underneath.

Saturday morning was winterly. The window panes were dripping wet and there was a coating of frost on my car in the courtyard. I wondered if I was still in Italy, but of course they also get winter here. After all *Mont Blanc* – or *Monte Bianca* – is only about 100 kilometres away with its peak visible in the distance. Franco Rovero picked me up and we drove towards Silvano d'Orba on the *autostrada*. We were periodically enveloped by a thick *nebbia* – the famous mist that gives its name to the grape variety Nebbiolo which obviously thrives in the fine water vapour. We began by visiting *il sindaco* in the town hall – the mayor Giuseppe Cocco – who would also attend the seminar: *Il futuro della grappa artiginale di qualità*. (The future of the boutique quality grappa.)

The seminar – which was held in the magnificent Villa Bottaro – for me of course was a heaven sent gift. The mayor introduced the seminar, marketing consultants extolled the importance of grappa for the region and local artisan distillers explained their production methods and defined the major differences between themselves and industrial producers. Suggestions were discussed as to the definition of a "quality grappa" and labelling rules were put forward and debated. Luckily, I also received notes from the seminar to study later.

Afterwards we were served an appetizer and white wine at a desk in the great hall. I was hungry, obviously, because I did not notice the shiny white laid tables when I tried to fill myself up on small very tasty *crostini*. Dinner was a masterly performance in the art of *slow food* – a sensory symphony composed by a *maestro* in the same class as Beethoven. The food defied description – or at least required the penmanship of Shakespeare.

For example I was told that the one of the cheeses that was served – the ancient *Montebore* – had fallen into obscurity twenty to thirty years ago, but that a slow food enthusiast had managed to find an old woman – the only one living who still knew how to make it. Today, the cheese is a success for the producers. Essentially, *slow food* is about enjoying the food of the surrounding area, enjoying the flavours that characterizes the region.

After dinner a field trip to the antique distillers in the middle of Silvano d'Orba was arranged for the guests – *Distilleria (Bartolomeo e Susanna) Gualco* and *Antica Distilleria Artigiana (di S. de Palo e) L. Barile*. We also received a lesson from the respective *maestri*, Alessandro Soldatini and Luigi Barile in the art of producing a genuine grappa. Both distilleries use the method *discontinuo a bagnomaria*.

On the way to San Marzanotto, Franco and I chatted. He did not speak English but was good at speaking in slow Italian. By speaking slowly myself I could keep up a fairly fluent conversation. And when I could not find the proper word, I just took the English word and "Italified" it. It worked remarkably often.

DISTILLERIA GUALCO
GRAPPA DI DOLCETTO D'OVADA
– GIOVANE –

ANTICA DIST. BARILE
GRAPPA DI DOLCETTO
– GIOVANE –

The rediscovered long gone cheese Montebore that was named "The Jurassic cheese" by American media.

Quality grappa – proposed definitions

Saturday the 19th of November 2005 a grappa seminar was held at Villa Bottaro in the town of Silvano d'Orba in Piemonte. The choice of locale was not by chance, Silvano d'Orba is renowned for its "antique" distilleries that distil with traditional equipment. Beside the local master-distillers, the mayor Guiseppe Coco, representatives from the local municipality and participants from the food and beverage industry all attended. The moderator was Maurizio Fava, senior lecturer of *slow food* and Italian distillates. On the agenda the question was raised of the future of small-scale manufacture of "quality grappa" and how this can be defined more precisely.

Today, anyone can call a grappa a "quality grappa". The term is neither consistently defined nor protected. The need for such a definition varies between distilleries, fillers, bottlers and other grappa sales people. One group that would certainly benefit from a clear stamp of quality are the artisan distillers – they have the best opportunity to create a "quality grappa". However, there is one category that is a thousand time larger, far more important and would definitely benefit from quality certification – grappa consumers. They love grappa and want to learn more about grappa. They support the entire foundation of the industry. The customers have the right to know what they are buying.

Interest in grappa grows with knowledge as well as faith in the distilleries and other industry players. This is a prerequisite if grappa is going to be an alternative to the real giants in the market: cognac, whiskey, rum etc. The question remains whether the industry can meet this competition in the future without defining the terms of a quality product and provide the consumer with complete insight through clear labelling. Cognac, whisky and ouzo are, for example, required by law to be distilled *a discontinuo*.

Standing, from left: moderator Maurizio Fava (2nd), Franco Rovero (3rd), Guiseppe Coco, the mayor (6th). Sitting, from left: Luigi Barile, Laura Mazzetti, Allesandro Soldatini (4th).

Proposed definitions of quality "Denominazione comunale di origine grappa di Silvano"

- Certified and quality controlled
- Guaranteed unique
- Known origin of vinaccia from Gavi and Alto Monferrato area
- Traceability within production
- Artigianale – boutique grappa manufactured *a bagnomaria* in Piemonte without "demetylizer column" ("rectification")

Proposed alternative division of grappa*

- **Grappa** – Italian distillate from Italian vinaccia (grape solids)
- **Grappa artigianale** – grappa from selected vinaccia distilled by limited batch (*a discontinuo*)
- **Grappa industriale** – grappa from blended vinaccia using continuous distillation methods
- **Grappa fasulla**** – false grappa, produced outside of Italy or from imported vinaccia

Proposed labelling requirements

- If only one grape variety is used (*grappa monovitigno*) the variety and region should be noted
- the distillery's name, region and possibly even the distiller's name, also when grappa is bottled by non distilling wineries and farms.
- Date of distilling and bottling
- Any added colourants
- Any added aromatic substances
- Any added sweeteners

* Presented by Maurizio Fava.
** Also included are grappa coloured with additives to give the impression of ageing in wooden barrels; and artisan grappa produced by industrial methods.

Top: From Distilleria Gualco.
Middle: Antica Distilleria L. Barile.
Left: Luigi Barile and Saveria de Palo.
Right: Alessandro Soldatini (Dist. Gualco).

The night was cold, the coldest up until that point. I woke several times and tried to preserve my warmth by curling up into a fetal position. I wondered how cold a foot could become before it would fall off. At that moment I was convinced that houses like this just could not burn. I was also convinced that I needed to move. In the morning, I easily leaped out into the corridor and in the shower. The bathroom billowed smoke like a distillery. The breakfast area looked magical in the sunshine but when I stepped out into the courtyard I saw a fireman on the roof. A fireman! The chimney was alight but the house was fine – but still, it was a fire. The fire truck with ladder and all was parked on the street outside.

I went to meet with Franco Rovero to get some help arranging visits with distilleries in the area. Afterwards I headed north full of expectation. I crossed the *autostrada* and drove on instinct because I wanted to be surprised by the beautiful landscape and dreamily desolate villages like Callianao, Grana and Montemegna on the way towards Altavilla Monferrato, where both Antica Distilleria Laura Mazzetti and Distilleria Mazzetti d'Altavilla are situated.

ANTICA DISTILLERIA
LAURA MAZZETTI
GRAPPA DI BARBERA
– *INVECCHIATA* –

Antica Distilleria Laura Mazzetti

This distillery also includes a grappa museum. *Maestra* Laura Mazzetti gave a tour of the facility where the action was. At the boiler she motioned for me to walk around the pile of exhausted vinaccia on the ground. A man was raking the pile when it suddenly dissolved and exposed a scary hole – like a big mouth glowing with fire. It was the fire flames for the boiler. In that hole you tread only once, I thought. The *alambicco* was a genuine antique using the *discontinuo a vapore diretto* process. The museum was surprisingly large, considering the exterior, and offered historically interesting equipment as well as a beautiful rustic tiled environment and a tastefully displayed exhibition.

Maestra Laura Mazzetti.   *From the museum and the exhibition.*

Distilleria Mazzetti d'Altavilla
Mazzetti d'Altavilla and Distilleria di Laura Mazzetti are two competitors in the same city with a common origin – Filippo Mazzetti who founded a distillery in 1846 in the town of Montemagno. Today the Mazzetti d'Altavilla is the leading grappa producer and exporter in Piemonte and one of the most prominent in Italy. They offer an extensive assortment of grappas in conspicuously elegant bottles and luxurious packages as well as extravagant accessories.

LATER ON THE WAY BACK TO THE PENSION I anticipated a cold evening in front of the computer. Maybe a drop of cold wine would warm me up but it was the work that I hoped would generate the heat. When I opened the door to my room I stumbled over a large fan heater and in the dining room I found a substantial infra-red heater. My host obviously had placed them there. As I had arrived direct from the light neon-blue *lavanderia* in Asti I hung up my three-quarters dry clothing around the heaters. The radiation heat did not quite manage to keep the room temperature up, but it still gave me enough warmth to work in peace and get a fairly good night's sleep. During the night the warm light from the heater swept over my bed, back and forth, regular and secure like a beacon.

Distilleria Beccaris

Distilleria Beccaris is located on a crossroads in the middle of the village Boglietto near Costigliole d'Asti, in an billowing area of the Muscat, Nebbiolo, Dolcetto, Barbera, Grignolino, Brachetto, Chardonnay and Cortese – all typical grape varieties for the wine districts south of Asti with names like Lauretum, Colli Astiani, Colline del Nizza, Castelli, Canelli e le terre d'oro. The white smoke signals from the distillery were like a landmark. The outside of the site is as charming as the interior.

The distillery was established in the early 1950's by Elio Beccaris and is now run by his son Carlo Beccaris and his family. One of the sons

DIST. BECCARIS
GRAPPA MOSCATO
– GIOVANE –

The tell tale sign of a distillery – white smoke. Distilleria Beccaris.

Drying used vinaccia to create fuel.

The boiler is fed constantly with vinaccia.

Beccaris' separate artisan style still.

is responsible for the excellent design of the Beccaris grappa bottles.

"We have just installed an *alambicco discontinuo a bagnomaria* to complement our continuous system," said Carlo Beccaris. It's for smaller series of *grappa monovitigno* from single wine producers. "One tonne of vinaccia is enough for a series, whereas our continuous processes demand between 20 and 40 tonnes. We buy it from local districts of Liguria such as Cinque Terre, Riviera di Levante, Riviera di Ponente, Albenga and Ortovero. Some also comes from Tuscany. There is a high demand amongst Italians for boutique-grappa and we want to be able to offer both."

"We distil around 4,000 tons of vinaccia during the season from October to February. After the first distillation the distillate has an alcohol content of around 20-25 percent. This so called *flemma* is concentrated in a column until the alcohol percentage reaches 70-80. It is then redistilled in a rectification column. This increases the alcohol content further to about 90-95 percent in order to remove methyl alcohol as *testa* and water and various higher alcohols as *coda*. The *testa* and *coda* are separated automatically and the *cuore* is tapped within the interval of 80-70 percent on the alcohol meter. I test the quality continuously. After the tap the grappa is cooled to minus 18°C and diluted with water to an alcohol strength of 40-42 percent."

"Our grappa is soft," he said. "*Morbida*. A Trentino grappa for example is drier *più secco*, more abrasive." I myself tasted the 80 percent *cuore* directly from the *alambicco*. *Maestro* Carlo did not reveal the strength beforehand, otherwise I probably would not have dared. Had he asked me to estimate the alcohol content, I would have said 50 percent.

"We are self-sufficient when it comes to energy," said Carlo Beccaris. "During the distilling process around 60 percent of the moisture in the raw product disappears which we afterwards dry and then reuse to produce steam and heat. The white smoke from the chimney is water

Distilleria Beccaris' alambicco a continuo. The steel column called "Colonna distillatrice" is used together with the "Colonna di concentrazione" – the copper part on top – to obtain the cuore. The middle column "Colonna degli oli" and the left "Colonna demetilatrice" are used for rectifying purposes when a distillate needs further cleaning.

Distilleria Beccaris in downtown Boglietto.

vapour from the drying process. Before we burn the vinaccia we separate out the seeds which then becomes the best cooking oil of all – *olio di vinacciolo* or *olio di semi d'uva*. Neutral in taste, rich in polyunsaturated Omega-6 fatty acids and antioxidants, with zero cholesterol and a very high flaming point of 180°C.

Distillerie Berta

After my visit at *Beccaris* I headed directly east through the vineyards that at last were allowed to recover after the intensive harvest season. Out there, amongst the rolling valleys in Casalotto di Mombaruzzo, is the impressively modern Distillerie Berta plant, which also includes a grappa museum. Previously they were situated in Nizza Monferrato.

Berta is an industrial producer and exporter with an annual production run of around one million bottles. If volume is any indication, there were 20,000 blue plastic vats of vinaccia, stored outside waiting to be distilled. My guide Elena Arzu explained that during the storage when the skins ferment a pressure is created by carbon dioxide within the container. The carbon dioxide was said to press the harmful oxygen out through a very tiny hole in the lid and prevent spoilage.

DISTILLERIA BERTA
*GRAPPA NIBBIO
– GIOVANE –*

Berta's new plant in Casalotto di Mombaruzzo.

The mosque inspired ageing cellar of more than 1800 m² (19,375 sq.ft), just before its completion in 2005.

Berta's grappas have labels bearing the names of pleasant sounding wines such as Moscato d'Asti, Barbera d'Asti, Nebbiolo da Barolo, Gavi and Brunello di Montalcino. Often they are aged in wooden barrels producing amber-toned grappa which sometimes approaches red. The distinct colours together with the bottle's refined shape makes you think of cognac. Berta's white grappa comes in a high bottle, shaped like a lighthouse, with a round knob on the top – a flashing landmark in liquor boutiques and bars world-over.

Distillerie Francoli

Distillerie Francoli is easy to find. Take the A26 from Alessandria – where it becomes one of Italy's finest and least busy *autostrade* – and exit at Ghemme. "Up here we see the A26 as our private highway," joked Alessandro Francoli, president and partner in the family business. *F.lli* in a corporate name means *fratelli*, brothers.

"Decisive for the grappa quality is the condition of the raw material and how you distil it," said Alessandro. "Nowadays, even industrial distilleries can make a high quality grappa with distinctive character, provided that the vinaccia is fresh and handled with care. In our continuous process we ensure that the vinaccia is constantly in motion so that the contact with the vapour is as brief and gentle as possible. To avoid undesired over extraction of volatile components the pressure of the steam is kept low, as is the temperature, around 104-105°C".

"Rectification, which is used by the industry, is needed only if the grape skins have gone bad from improper storage," said Alessandro. "That shouldn't be a problem anymore now that storage methods have greatly improved."

The use of sugar is a matter of taste and varies from company to company. "The law permits two percent," continued Alessandro.

DIST. FRANCOLI
*GRAPPA CRU
DI BRACHETTO
– GIOVANE –*

The shop of Francoli winery and distillery in Ghemme not far from Milan.

The freshness of vinaccia is crucial, says Alessandro Francoli.

"When you make a grappa *Moscato* or *Brachetto* no sugar is recommended since the grapes have a sweet character. Other grappas may improve by adding a small amount. 0.5 percent sugar is completely acceptable."

"However the use of other additives, for example food flavouring agents, I am completely against. It risks the existence of the genuine grappa – especially when larger and more influential producers use it. If we accept the use of these flavours the consumer may not know what the genuine grappa should taste like. Grappa would then be in danger

Alessandro Francoli's thesis for his degree in chemistry was the study of grappa ageing.

of being falsified and will eventually lose its unique individuality."

"We exclusively use vinaccia from local grape varieties such as Nebbiolo, Barbera, Muscat, Brachetto. After distilling the grape seeds are removed and used for producing grape-seed oil, the skins dried and reused as fuel for the distillation process and the heating of our plant. Our impact on the environment is minimal. Ecology and quality are my missions. Grappa producers should put more energy into this as well as focusing on grappa as a cultural drink with unique characteristics."

WHEN I LEFT THE DISTILLERIE FRANCOLI the sun had started to near the horizon and gradually transformed the right-side of the car window to a 19th century painting. The atmosphere stayed with me all the way to the *agriturismo* where I continued to work on the computer and listen to music. I had discovered Mozart's PIANO CONCERTO NO. 25 and let myself get swept away by that jubilant music that only he could compose. And that teasing development section with the Marseillaise-like upbeat that he breaks and holds back over and over again until the flood surges forth. And the surprisingly romantic element in the slow movement with the harmonies that must have inspired Chopin, when he had reached the climatic point in Krakoviak and searched for a heavenly way to come back down to Earth again.

Distilleria Marolo

Distilleria (Santa Maria F.lli) Marolo lies almost hidden away in a suburb of Alba, south west of Asti on the borderline between the Langhe and Monferrato wine districts. The high vaulted roof and the large reflective windows, that soak up the idyllic surroundings of the façade, gives the distillery a distinctly exclusive feel. It fits. Marolo's grappas are exclusive but in ways other than just the shape of the bottle. *Maestro* Paolo Marolo is a modern artisan who captures *cuore* with passion and consideration for tradition but also ventures into new techniques, product development

Distilleria Marolo in Alba.

DISTILLERIA MAROLO
GRAPPA DI BAROLO
– RISERVA –

DISTILLERIA MAROLO
GRAPPA DI BAROLO
– RISERVA –

and marketing. When I met Paolo I had no idea there was a connection. The situation was absurd, as this connection was the reason why I was in Italy in the first place. So when we wandered around the distillery and Paolo showed me the two *alambicchi a bagnomaria*, explained the difference between industrial and boutique grappa and told me about the acacia and oak barrels behind the tightly sealed storage areas, I did not yet sense any premonition at all.

We entered the *cantina* where Marolo's grappas were lined up: clean, simply designed bottles with expressive art deco inspired labels together with sophisticated pieces of art bottles and luxurious packaging of noble wood. *Grappe giovani* followed by second names like Moscato, Dolcetto, Brachetto, Barbaresco, Freisa, Gavi, Arneis, Brunello di Montalcino, Verdicchio Bucci. *Grappe invecchiate* with attributes like Barbera, Nebbiolo and Barolo. It was then that I caught sight of the little bird.

"Try this," said Paolo and poured up a *Grappa di Barolo*, aged for 15 years with an alcohol content of 50 percent. "Amber-coloured with a beautiful wooden barrel aroma towards vanilla, roasted almonds and chocolate," explained Paolo. I myself only found one word for it – enormous. But I could not let go of the little bird or rather the label and bottle it sat on. Where had I seen it before?

Suddenly it hit me, as when a flavour or aroma releases a chain of lightning fast associations. Except that it was not a flavour that prompted this reaction. I just realized that I in fact had tasted this grappa before – and dismissed it. I also realized that my trip was getting very near the end and that this was my last distillery visit.

The distilleries were running out of vinaccia, the season was over and it was time for me to think of a refrain. There I stood in Piemonte with a balloon of an excellent grappa *Grappa di Barolo* in my hand and meditated on it together with the *maestro* himself. Suddenly Ivo Dalpas

Maestro Paolo Marolo himself.

popped into my thoughts, the man with his modest still in his garage and his simple little shop in Trentino – my trip's first distillery whose coarse grappa had made me stagger in shock. Now I looked forward to trying Dalpas grappa at home in my living room. I knew I would enjoy it. I did not doubt it for a second. Because only a few moments ago I had tasted a *Grappa di Barolo*, with the little bird on, and I had loved it from the first sniff. Even though it was not a *grappa giovane* – that on my journey I discovered a preference for – but a *grappa invecchiata*. Even though I now realized that my memory of the bird came from my own home – from the bottle that my daughter had bought in Turin on the recommendation of a connoisseur. From the grappa that had puzzled me and whose name I had forgotten – and finally had made me get on the road to Grappaland to find out.

Two grappas: my trip's first and last – Dalpas' *Grappa Teroldego* and Marolo's *Grappa di Barolo*. One was in my hand, the other in my mind. The transformation they had undergone was enormous.

Yet they had not changed at all.

DISTILLERIA MAROLO
GRAPPA DI MOSCATO
– GIOVANE –

DISTILLERIA MAROLO
GRAPPA DI BARBARESCO
– GIOVANE –

References, sources and acknowledgements

ON GRAPPA

Grappa – tra assaggi e alambicchi
Luigi Odello.
Centro studi assaggiatori

Grappa – only Italian by tradition and by law
Istituto nazionale grappa
Centro studi assaggiatori

La grappa, i grappaioli e il grappaiol'angelico
Graziella D'agata e Elio Chiodi
Edizioni Acanthus

Grappa
Axel och Bibiana Behrendt
Wilhelm Heyne Verlag GmbH & Co,
Abbeville Press

La grappa veneta – uomini, alambicchi e sapori dell'antica terra dei Dogi
Domenico Musumarra
Vininviaggio

Tuscan grappa and the masters of time
Andrea Zanfi
Carlo Cambi Editore

Libellus de aqua ardenti
Michaellis Savonarola. Pisa 1484
Ars Antiqua editrice Milano

Le grappe di Luigi Barile
Virgilio Pronzati
A modo mio – i libelluli

A guide to the discovery of grappa
Poli Museo della Grappa, Bassano del Grappa
Distillerie Poli

ON WINE

Vin
André Dominé
Könemann Tandem Verlag GmbH, Königswinter

Vin – vinet och druvorna
Andreas Kjörling
Grenadine Bokförlag

Vinguiden
Fiona Sims
Parragon

OTHER

www.wikipedia – the free encyclopedia

www.shenet.se – a Swedish information service on skin care, perfumery and aroma therapy.

Italiano. Corso preparativo I - II
Univerb language courses

Picture, page 47 – Elena Arzu, Distillerie Berta

Musical illustration, page 65 – Chopin, Klavierwerke Band I. Edition Peters

Gioacchino Nannoni, page 132 – quotation based on "Tuscan grappa and the masters of time" by Andrea Zanfi

Romano Levi, page 147 – text based on www.grapparomanolevi.it (Giorgio Toso)

I WOULD LIKE TO THANK

Bruno Pilzer at *Distilleria Pilzer*, moreover teacher at *Istituto Agrario di San Michele all'Adige* in Trentino, for the initial grappa lesson and scientific insight into the processes within the alambicco.

Alessandro Francoli at *Distillerie Francoli* for the generous disposal of expert competence during the completion of La Scuola.

Maurizio Fava – grappa and slow-food connoisseur – for the tangible support and encouragement during the entire development of the project.

Gunnar Hall – neighbour and doctor in aroma chemistry – for checking passages regarding the content of grappa and tasting in general.

Elin and **Jonty Bogardus** – my eldest daughter and son-in-law – for the persistent scrutinizing and fine tuning of the language in the international edition.

Annie Boudin – my second daughter – for checking the Italian expressions, and my treating of Italy on the whole.

Karin Boudin – my beloved wife – for her heartfelt support of my somewhat eccentric and very solitary grappa project.

Finally I would like to express my gratitude to my friend and co-worker – art director **Anders Wallin** – for his devotion and patience, and above all because the book's design and feeling truly express that very soul of the grappa I was looking for.

List of grappa distilleries

● **Artisan grappa distillery** that uses a batch-wise method (*a discontinuo*). In connection with an industrial-size distillery this symbol indicates that it has, to some extent, a separate equipment for the production of boutique grappa.

■ **Industrial-size distillery** that mainly uses a continuous distillation system (*a continuo*) or buys and blend grappa, or both.

No symbol indicates that the distilling method is unknown.

Reservation. The list is based on various sources and may contain inaccurate information regarding corporate details and distilling methods.

Roner Distillerie ■ ●
Josef-von-Zallinger Str.44
39040 Termeno/Tramin (BZ)
www.roner.com
info@roner.com

Distilleria Privata Unterthurner ●
Via Anselm Pattis 14, 39020 Marling (BZ)
www.unterthurner.it
info-dist@unterthurner.it

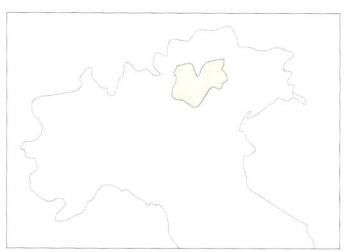

TRENTINO

Distilleria Angeli Sergio ■ ●
Via Capitelli 11, 38074 Dro (TN)
grappangeli@hotmail.it

Distilleria Bailoni Vittorio ●
Via Crucis 5, 38049 Vigolo Vattaro (TN)
distilleria.bailoni@tin.it

Distilleria Bertagnolli ■ ●
Via del Teroldego, 11/13
38016 Mezzocorona (TN)
www.bertagnolli.it
info@bertagnolli.it

Distilleria Bresciani Ernesto ●
Località Fontanelle, 38068 Tenno (TN)

Distilleria Dalpas Ivo ●
Località Castelletto 4, 38010 Ton (TN)

Distilleria Fedrizzi ●
Via Giuseppe Verdi, 8
38010 Toss di Ton (TN)

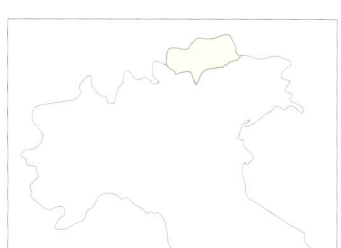

ALTO ADIGE

Distilleria Alfons Walcher ●
Via Pillhof 99, 39057 Frangarto/Appiano (BZ)
www.walcher.eu
info@brennerei-walcher.com

Cantina Sociale Lagundo/Kellerei Algund ●
Via Portici 218, 39012 Merano (BZ)

Distilleria Psenner L. ■ ●
Via Stazione 1, 39040 Tramin (BZ)
www.psenner.com
info@psenner.com

Distilleria Giacomozzi Renzo & Figli 🟢
Loc. Stedro 12, 38047 Segonzano (TN)

**Distilleria Istituto Agrario
di San Michele all'Adige** 🟢
Via Edmondo Mach, 1
38010 San Michele all'Adige (TN)
www.ismaa.it
cantina@ismaa.it

Distilleria Marzadro 🟥 🟢
Via per Brancolino, 10
38060 Nogaredo (TN)
www.marzadro.it
info@marzadro.it

Distilleria Paolazzi Vittorio 🟢
Via Vich 27, 38030 Faver (TN)
m.paolazzi@virgilio.it

Distilleria Pezzi Fabio 🟥
Piazza Santa Barbara, 6
38010 Campodenno (TN)
distilleriapezzi@virgilio.it

Distilleria Pilzer 🟢
Via Portegnago 5, 38030 Faver (TN)
www.pilzer.it
info@pilzer.it

Distilleria F.lli Pisoni 🟢
Via San Siro 7/a, Pergolese di Lassino
38070 Sarche (TN)
www.pisoni.net
info@pisoni.net

Azienda Agricola Pojer e Sandri 🟢
Via Molini 4, 38010 Faedo (TN)
www.pojeresandri.it
info@pojeresandri.it

Distilleria Casimiro di Bernardino Poli 🟢
Fraz. S. Massenza 43, 38070 Vezzano (TN)
bernardinopoli@alice.it
www.distilleriacasimiro.it

Distilleria Francesco Poli 🟢
Fraz. S. Massenza 36, 38070 Vezzano (TN)
www.francescopoli.it
francescopoli@francescopoli.it

Distilleria Giovanni Poli & Figli 🟢
Fraz. S. Massenza, Via del Lago, 3
38070 Vezzano (TN)
www.poligiovanni.it
info@poligiovanni.it

Distilleria Mauro e Giulio Poli 🟢
Fraz. Santa Massenza
38070 Vezzano (TN)
info@valeriopoli.it

Distilleria Valerio Poli 🟢
Frazione Santa Massenza
38070 Vezzano (TN)
info@valeriopoli.it

Distilleria Pravis 🟢
Località Le Biolche, 1
38076 Lasino (TN)
www.pravis.it
info@pravis.it

Distilleria Segnana F.lli Lunelli 🟢
Via del Ponte di Ravina 13, 38040 Trento
www.ferrarispumante.it
info@ferrarispumante.it

Distilleria Tranquillini 🟢
Località Noreda 1, 38062 Arco (TN)

Distilleria Vettorazzi 🟢
Corso Centrale, 11
38056 Levico Terme (TN)
www.grappavettotazzi.it
info@grappavettorazzi.it

Distilleria Villa de Varda 🟥 🟢
38017 Mezzolombardo (TN)
www.villadevarda.com
info@villadevarda.com

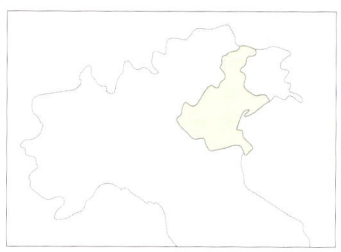

VENETO

Distillerie Bonollo Umberto 🟥
Via Galileo Galilei 6, 35035 Mestrino (PD)
www.bonollo.it
info@bonollo.it

Distilleria Bottega 🟥 🟢
Via Galileo Galilei, 11
31020 Castello Roganzuolo di Sab Fior (TV)
www.alexander.it
info@alexander.it

Distilleria F.lli Brunello 🟢
Via Giuseppe Roi 51, 36047 Montegalda (VI)
www.brunello.it
info@brunello.it

Brotto Distillerie
Via XXX Aprile 11, 31041 Cornuda (TV)
www.brotto.it
brottodistillerie@brotto.it

Azienda Agricola di Capovilla Vittorio 🟢
Via Giardini, 12-1
36027 Rosà (VI)
capovilladistillati@virgilio.it

**Distilleria Acquavite
(Roberto Castagner)** 🟥 🟢
Via Bosco 25, 31028 Visnà di Vazzola (TV)
www.robertocastagner.it
info@robertocastagner.it

Distilleria Centopercento 🟢
Via A. Carretta, 19/C
31040 Nervesa della Battaglia (TV)
info@centopercento.net
www.centopercento.net

Distilleria Franceschini 🟢
Strada del Trenin, 50
37010 Cavaion Veronese (VR)
www.distilleriafranceschini.it
distilleriafranceschini@virgilio.it

Distilleria Artigiana Gobetti Carlo 🟢
Via Ghiandare, 14
37010 Marciaga di Costermano (VR)

Distilleria Le Crode 🟢
Via Masetti 11, 32030 Vas (BL)
www.distillerialecrode.com
info@distillerialecrode.com

Distilleria Maschio Beniamino
Via San Michele, 70
31020 San Pietro di Feletto (TV)
www.conegliano.com
maschio.beniamino@conegliano.com

Distilleria Maschio Bonaventura 🟥 🟢
Via Vizza 6, 31018 Gaiarine (TV)
www.primeuve.com
info@primeuve.com

Maschio Pietro & figli Distilleria
Via Cappuccini, 18
37032 Monteforte d´Alpone (VR)

Distilleria Milanese 🟥
Via Calmaor 18, 31020 S. Vendemmiano (TV)

Distilleria Nardini 🟥
Ponte Vecchio 2, 36061 Bassano del Grappa (VI)
www.nardini.it
nardini@nardini.it

Distilleria Andrea da Ponte 🟥
Via 1° maggio 1, 31020 Corbanese di Tarzo (TV)
www.daponte.it
info@daponte.it

Poli Distillerie 🟥 🟢
Via Marconi 46, 36060 Schiavon (VI)
(The museum is in Bassano del Grappa)
www.poligrappa.com
info@poligrappa.com

Distilleria Antonio Scaramellini 🟢
(*a fuoco diretto*)
Via Garibaldi 48, 37010 Sandrà (VR)
www.distilleria-scaramellini.com
info@distilleria-scaramellini.com

Distilleria Schiavo 🟢
Via Mazzini 39, 36030 Costabissara (VI)
www.schiavograppa.com
info@schiavograppa.com

Scuola Enologica di Conegliano 🟢
www.scuolaenologica.it
info@scuolaenologica.it

Distilleria F.lli Caffo/Distiladôr del Friûl
Via San Daniele, 9
33037 Passons di Pasian di Prato (UD)
www.grappafriulana.it
dist.friuli@caffo.com

Distilleria Giacomo Ceschia 🟢
33045 Nimis (UD)
www.ceschia.it
ceschia@ceschia.it

Distilleria Domenis 🟢
Via Darnazzacco 30, 33043 Cividale del Friuli(UD)
www.domenis.it
info@domenis.it

Nonino Distillatori 🟢
Via Aquileia 104, 33050 Percoto (UD)
info@nonino.it
www.nonino.it

Distilleria D. Pagura di Lindo Pagura & C. 🟢
Via Favetti 25, 33080 Castions di Zoppola (UD)
www.distilleriapagura.com

Distillerie Bepi Tosolini 🟥 🟢
Marsure di Povoletto(UD)
info@bepitosolini.it
www.bepitosolini.it

Distilleria Az. Agr. Tenuta Villanova 🟢
Via Contessa Berettta, 29
34070 Villanova di farra(GO)

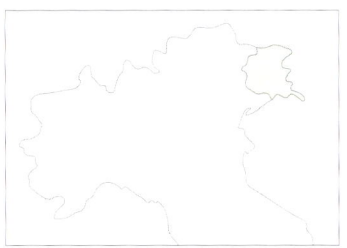

FRIULI – VENEZIA GIULIA

Distilleria Aquileia 🟥
Via Julia Augusta 87/A, 33051 Aquileia (UD)
www.distilleriaaquileia.com

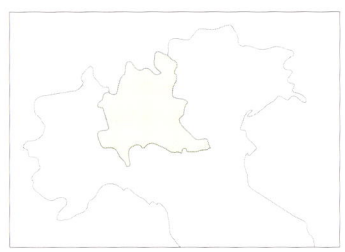

LOMBARDY

Bianchini G. Di Gianolini Vittorio & C. 🟢
Via Nazionale 17, 23012 Castione Andevenno (SO)

Azienda Agricola Conti Terzi
Via Sopramura 8, 25038 Rovato (BS)
www.agricolacontiterzi.it
contiterzi@libero.it
agricolacontiterzi@virgilio.it

Distillerie Locatelli Fabrizio 🟥
Via Scotti 2, 24030 Mapello (BG)

Distillerie Franciacorta 🟥
Via Mandalossa 80, 25064 Gussago (BS)
www.distilleriefranciacorta.it
info@distilleriefranciacorta.it

Distillerie Peroni Maddalena 🟢
Via Alcide de Gasperi 39, 25064 Gussago (BS)
www.distillerieperoni.com
info@distillerieperoni.com

Cantina Storica di Montù Beccaria 🟢
Via Marconi 10, 27040 Montù Beccaria (PV)
www.ilmontu.com
ilmontu@ilmontu.com

Distillerie Frassine PierGiulio 🟢
Via Caporalino 7, 25064 Gussago (BS)

Distillerie Pirotelli 🟥
Via Mazzini Giuseppe 15, 25086 Rezzato (BS)

Distilleria F.lli Ramazzotti 🟥
20020 Lainate, Lombardia

Distillatori Rossi d'Angera 🟢
Via Puccini 20, 21021 Angera (VA)
www.rossidangera.com
info@rossidangera.com

Distillerie Sari di Saleri 🟥
Via Sale 145, 25064 Gussago (BS)

Distillerie Riunite Schenatti – Della Morte 🟢
Via Martiri della Libertà 1, 23037 Tirano (SO)
www.schenatti.com
info@schenatti.com

Cantina Sociale La versa 🟥 🟢
Via F Crispi 15, 27047 S. Maria della Versa (PV)
www.laversa.it
info@laversa.it

Distilleria La Valtellinese – Invitti Enrico 🟥
Via L. Mallero Cadorna 68, 23100 Sondrio (SO)
enrico@tiscalinet.com

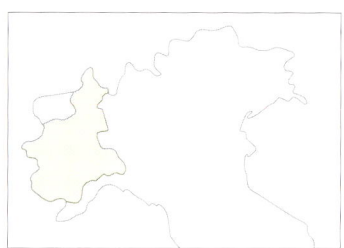

PIEMONTE

**Antica Distilleria di Altavilla
di Laura Raimondo Mazzetti** 🟢
Loc. Cittadella 1, 15041 Altavilla Monferrato (AL)
www.altavilla.com
info@altavilla.com

**Antica Distilleria artigiana
di S. de Palo e L. Barile** 🟢
Via Roccagrimalda 17,15060 Silvano d'Orba(Al)
grappa.barile@tele2.it

A.G.B. Antica Grapperia Bosso 🟢
Località Stazione 5, 14026 Cunico (AT)
www.grappabosso.it
info@grappabosso.it

Distilleria del Barbaresco 🟥
Località Bricco Albano 1, 2050 Barbaresco (CN)
Dist.barbaresco@tiscalinet.it

Distilleria Beccaris Elio 🟥 🟢
Via Alba 5, Frazione Boglietto
14056 Costigliole d'Asti (AT)
www.distilleriabeccaris.it
info@distilleriabeccaris.it

Distillerie Berta 🟥
Via Guasti 34-36, Frazione Casalotto
14046 Mombaruzzo (AT)
www.distilleriaberta.it
info@distilleriaberta.it

Distilleria Bocchino 🟥 🟢
Via Giovanni Battista Giuliani, 88
14053 Canelli (AT)
www.bocchino.it
info@bocchino.it

Distilleria Castelli Guiseppe 🟥
Corso L. Einaudi 55, 12074 Cortemilia (CN)
distilleriacastelli@tiscali.it
distcastelli@libero.it

Distilleria Ceretto 🟢
Località Brunate, 12064 La Morra (CN)
www.ceretto.com
ceretto@ceretto.com

Della valle Distilleria
Via Tiglione 1, 14040 Vigliano d'Asti
distilleria@robertodellavalle.191.it

Distillerie Francoli 🟥 🟢
C.so Romagnano 20, 28074 Ghemme (NO)
www.francoli.it
francoli@francoli.it

Distilleria Gualco 🟢
Via XX settembre 3, 15060 Silvano d'Orba (AL)
www.distilleriagualco.it
info@distilleriagualco.it

Levi Romano 🟢
(*a fuoco diretto*)
Località Borgonuovo, 12052 Neive (CN)

Distilleria Magnoberta di Luparia Alberto 🟢
Via Asti 6, 15033 Casale Monferrato (AL)
www.magnoberta.com
info@magnoberta.com

Distilleria Santa Teresa dei Fratelli Marolo 🟢
Corso canale 105, Mussotto 12051 Alba (CN)
www.marolo.com
grappe@marolo.com

Mazzetti d'Altavilla – Distillatori dal 1846 🟥 🟢
Viale Unità d'Itali, 2
15041 Altavilla Monferrato (AL)
www.mazzetti.it

Distilleria dr. M. Montanaro 🟢
Via Garibaldi 6, 12060 Gallo di Grizzane (CN)
www.distilleriemontanaro.com
distilleriemontanaro@libero.it

Distilleria F.lli Revel Chion 🟥
Via Casassa 4, 10010 Chiaverano (TO)
www.distilleria-revelchion.it
info@distilleria-revelchion.it

Azienda Rovero 🟢
Frazione San Marzanotto, 216
Località Valdonata, 14100 Asti (AT)
www.rovero.it
info@rovero.it

**Distilleria Cooperativa
Rosignano – Cellamonte** 🟢
Via Isola 2, 15030 Rosignano Monferrato (AL)

Distilleria Sibona 🟢
Loc. Buonagiunta 1/a, 12040 Piobesi d'Alba (CN)
www.distilleriasibona.it
info@distilleriasibona.it

Distilleria S. Tommaso 🟥
Reg. Guatrasone 99,
15046 San Salvatore Monferrato (AL)
www.santommaso-grappa.it
info@santommaso-grappa.it

Torino Distillati 🟥
Via Montegrappa 37, 10024 Moncalieri (TO)
tordist@tin.it

Distilleria Villa Rosati 🟥
Via Gallo 38, 12052 Neive (CN)

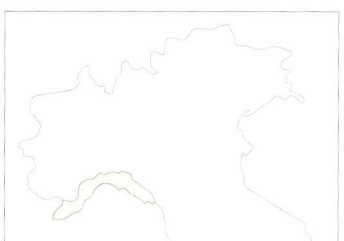

LIGURIA

Anticha Distilleria DiPortofino 🟢
Via G. Garibaldi 8, 16040 Ne (GE)
www.fratelliparma.it
filiparm@tin.it

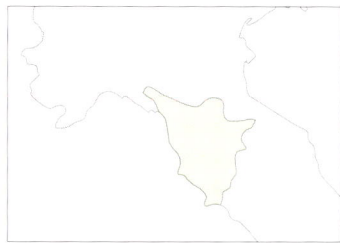

TUSCANY

Distilleria Nannoni 🟢
Via Aratrice 35, 58045 Civitella Paganico (SI)
www.nannoni.it
nannoni@nannoni.it

Distillerie Bonollo 🟥 🟢
Località Greti, 50022 Greve in Chianti (FI)
www.bonollo.com

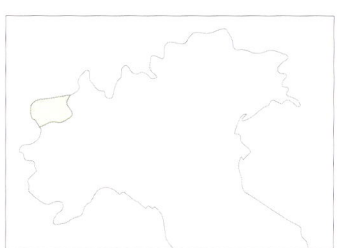

VALLE D'AOSTA

La Valdôtaine 🟢
11020 Saint Marcel (AO)